Tales of the Caribbean:
Supernatural Beings and Legendary Creatures

Connor G. Porter Taylor

Introduction

In the colorful and exuberant lands of the Caribbean, where the sun embraces paradisiacal beaches and the breeze carries with it the essence of history and traditions, there are supernatural beings and creatures that have inhabited the hearts and minds of its inhabitants for centuries. These creatures, wrapped in a halo of mystery and charm, have been the protagonists of countless myths and legends that have been passed down from generation to generation, weaving a rich and fascinating web of Caribbean folklore.

This book, "Tales of the Caribbean: Supernatural Beings and Legendary Creatures", was born from the deep admiration and curiosity for these fantastic figures that inhabit the collective imagination of the region. As researchers and writers of myths and legends, we have set out to explore, unravel and share with you the most captivating tales and the most intriguing stories of these creatures that have left an indelible mark on Caribbean culture.

The motivation behind this project is twofold. On the one hand, we are driven by the desire to preserve and value the cultural heritage of the Caribbean islands, where orality and tradition are fundamental pillars of identity. As time progresses and modernity takes over, it is crucial that we do not forget the stories that have nurtured our beliefs and have transmitted ancestral teachings to us. Through the collection of these legends, we hope to keep the flame of tradition alive and promote a sense of rootedness and belonging in Caribbean communities.

On the other hand, we are moved by the desire to share with the entire world the rich legacy of supernatural creatures that inhabit the Caribbean islands. We firmly believe in the power of stories to unite people, transcend borders and open the doors of the imagination. In a globalized world, where cultures converge and intertwine, it is essential to celebrate the diversity and uniqueness of every corner of the planet. Through this book, we invite readers from all latitudes to immerse themselves in the fascinating Caribbean narratives and discover the richness of these mythological creatures that connect us with a deeper and more magical dimension of existence.

The idea for this book stems from our passion for research and love of writing. We have spent countless hours immersed in libraries, interviewing scholars, and traversing the remotest corners of Caribbean islands in search of the most captivating and authentic stories. Each page of this book is the result of hard research, enthusiastic conversations with popular storytellers, and a deep respect for Caribbean beliefs and traditions.

Throughout these pages, we will enter the domains of the Ciguapas, those seductive creatures with inverted feet; we will meet the tempting Devils that awaken the darkest desires of men. We will discover the mysterious Jumbies, wandering spirits that lurk in the dark of night, and we will face the terrifying Lagahoos, men turned into furry beasts.

We cannot forget the presence of the Loogaroos, bloodthirsty Caribbean vampires, who soar the night skies in search of their prey. We will also meet Mama Dlo, the enigmatic siren of rivers and lakes, whose song attracts the unwary and plunges them into an uncertain destiny.

In our pages, we will meet the Bacá, protecting the community with their imposing presence. We will come across the Soucouyants, witches who shed their skin to become balls of fire and drink the blood of the unsuspecting.

We will also come across Tata Duende, the guardian spirit of the forests, with his hat and inverted feet, protecting nature and punishing those who harm it. And, of course, we can't forget Ti Malice, the cunning character who, with his pranks and pranks, teaches us lessons about morality and human mischief.

In each of these chapters, we'll dive into oral narratives and stories passed down from generation to generation. We will explore its origin, its symbolism and its impact on the daily life of Caribbean communities. Through the written word, we will bring these creatures to life, sharing their stories and revealing the secrets behind their legends.

This book is an invitation to a journey through the darkest and most enchanting paths of the Caribbean. Through these pages, we hope to arouse curiosity, admiration, and wonder for these supernatural creatures and beings that connect us with our roots and invite us to explore the magic and mystery of the Caribbean region.

Immerse yourself in the pages of "Caribbean Tales: Supernatural Beings and Legendary Creatures" and let yourself be enveloped by the seduction of the Devilesses, the mystery of the Jumbies and the wisdom of Tata Duende. Discover a fascinating universe that will transport you beyond the imaginable and will remind you of the importance of preserving our most precious traditions and beliefs.

Join us on this unforgettable journey through the myths and legends of the Caribbean and let yourself be captivated by the magic that only these creatures can offer!

Chapter 6: Mama Dlo
- The mysterious and enchanting Caribbean mermaid
- Tales of fishermen and boaters who have sighted Mama Dlo
- The duality of its nature and its consequences
- Modern adaptations in film or television related to Mama Dlo

Chapter 7: The Bacá
- The symbolism and meaning behind El Bacá
- Tales and stories of Bacá
- How to seize a Bacá
- Modern adaptations in film or television related to the Moko jumbies
Chapter 8: Soucouyant
- The profile and characteristics of the fearsome Soucouyant witches
- Legends and stories about the encounters with the Soucouyants
- Methods to protect yourself from Soucouyants according to popular tradition
- Modern adaptations in film or television related to the Soucouyants

Chapter 9: Tata Goblin
- The mythical guardian of the forests and his peculiar appearance
- Stories and anecdotes about the encounters with Tata Duende
- The role of Tata Duende in the protection of nature and animals
- Modern adaptations in film or television related to Tata Duende

Chapter 10: You Malice
Malice 's mischievous and cunning personality
- Anecdotes and tales illustrating their pranks and pranks
- The role of Ti Malice as a reflection of human cunning and its relationship to morality
- Modern adaptations in film or television related to Ti Malice

Conclusion:
- Reflection on the importance of supernatural beings and creatures in Caribbean folklore
- The cultural legacy and the preservation of these stories throughout generations
- Invitation to the reader to explore more about the folklore and traditions of the Caribbean

Appendix:
- Glossary of terms and vocabulary related to supernatural beings and creatures present in the book
- Additional resources for those interested in learning more about Caribbean folklore

This comprehensive index gives you an overview of what you'll find in the book! Each chapter delves into the essence of each supernatural being or creature, exploring its myths, legends, and modern adaptations in different audiovisual media. We are excited to share this fascinating journey through Caribbean folklore with you.

Chapter 1: Ciguapa

Origin and description of the Ciguapa

Ciguapas are legendary creatures originating from the Caribbean region, specifically the Dominican Republic and other surrounding areas. These fascinating creatures have a unique and charming appearance that has captured the imagination of people for generations.

While the exact story of their origin is uncertain due to their folkloric nature, there are historical records and references in literature that mention the Ciguapas. For example, in the book "Natural and Moral History of the Indies" written by the Dominican friar Bartolomé de las Casas in the 16th century, a brief mention is made of Ciguapas as mythical beings with upside-down feet.

The physical description of the Ciguapas is a notable characteristic of these creatures. They are said to have long dark hair that falls to their feet, luminous brown skin, and inverted feet. Their backward feet allow them to walk gracefully and deftly across the mountainous terrain, confusing those who try to follow in their footsteps. This physical peculiarity has been transmitted throughout the centuries in the legends and oral stories of the Caribbean region.

Although the appearance of the Ciguapas may vary slightly according to different local narratives and traditions, their uniqueness lies in their ability to attract and captivate those who observe them. The exotic and enigmatic beauty of Ciguapas has been described as hypnotic, capable of enchanting those who cross its path. Their long dark hair, combined with their glowing skin and inverted feet, make them fascinating and mysterious beings.

Some historical sources also suggest that the figure of the Ciguapa may have its origin in the beliefs and myths of the indigenous cultures that inhabited the Caribbean region before the arrival of the Europeans. These cultures had a close relationship with nature and believed in the existence of supernatural beings and guardians of the forests and mountains. Ciguapas could have emerged as a symbolic representation of this ancestral connection with the earth and natural elements.

Although the myth of the Ciguapas has endured over time, it is important to note that their existence is based on legends and oral traditions passed down from generation to generation. For many, Ciguapas are mystical and enchanting creatures that are part of the rich cultural heritage of the Caribbean, and their presence continues to inspire the imagination and wonder of those who hear their stories.

Although Ciguapas are creatures specific to the Caribbean region, there are some interesting similarities to other legendary creatures from different cultures around the world. Although these similarities can vary, it is fascinating to observe how certain aspects of legends and myths are intertwined in different traditions.

Here are some possible connections between Ciguapas and other legendary creatures: Mermaids: In various cultures, mermaids are depicted as beautiful aquatic women with a seductive voice. Like the Ciguapas, mermaids captivate humans with their charm and beauty, but they can also represent danger and deceit.
Lamias: In Greek mythology, lamias were female beings with the upper body of a woman and the lower body of a sea monster.

Like Ciguapas, lamias have a dual appearance, combining attractive and menacing elements.

Nymphas: In Roman mythology, nymphs were female spirits associated with nature and forests. Like the Ciguapas, the nymphs were known for their beauty and their ability to communicate with the natural elements.

Huldra: In Scandinavian legends, the Huldras are beautiful and alluring female beings who inhabit the forests. Like Ciguapas, Huldras can have peculiar physical features, such as a fox tail or tree trunk instead of a back.
The Banshees: In Irish mythology, the Banshees are female spirits that are associated with death and fate. Like the Ciguapas, the Banshees have an attractive appearance but can also be the bearer of bad news and dire omens.

These connections can provide an interesting perspective on how legendary creatures often share similar characteristics in different cultures. Although each of these creatures has its own history and cultural context, it is exciting to discover the common threads that run through myths and legends around the world.

Stories and legends about the Ciguapa

Ciguapas has been the subject of numerous stories and legends throughout the history of the Caribbean region. These stories, passed down orally from generation to generation, have contributed to the rich cultural and folkloric tradition of the area. Next, we will explore some of the most outstanding stories about the Ciguapas:

The Encounter with a Wandering Hunter: One of the best-known stories relates the encounter of a hunter with a Ciguapa deep in the forest. According to the story, the hunter entered the territory of the Ciguapas without knowing it and was captivated by the beauty of one of them. Fascinated by her charm, he followed in her footsteps without realizing that he was being led further and further from his original path. After a while, he realized that he was completely lost and disoriented. The Ciguapa mysteriously disappeared, leaving the hunter alone and confused in the middle of the forest.

The Protection Pact: According to a legend, the Ciguapas have a secret pact with the spirits of the forests and mountains. These creatures are said to fiercely protect the flora and fauna of the Caribbean region and punish those who break the laws of nature. In the story, a greedy man decided to indiscriminately cut down trees in the Ciguapas' territory to sell the wood.

Because of his greed, the man was chased by a flock of ominous birds and got lost in the woods, unable to find his way back. The Myth of Impossible Love: A popular legend tells the story of a young man who fell madly in love with a Ciguapa. Attracted by her beauty, the young man tried to woo her and convince her to leave her life in the woods to live by his side. However, Ciguapa explained that her destiny was linked to nature and she could not leave her home. Despite his sincere love, the young man realized that he could not change the nature of things and had to accept that his love was impossible.

The Warning to Hunters: In this story, it tells how the Ciguapas warn hunters about the dangers of indiscriminate hunting and the lack of respect for wildlife. Some Ciguapas are said to introduce themselves to daredevil hunters and warn them of the consequences of their actions. These mystical apparitions and the cryptic messages of the Ciguapas urge hunters to rethink their actions and respect the natural balance of the forest.

These stories and legends offer a fascinating insight into the relationship between Ciguapas and humans, as well as their role as guardians of nature.

Although Ciguapas are specific to the Caribbean region and Arabian myths have their own creatures and legends, there are some thematic similarities that can be found in both contexts. These similarities can be explored to highlight certain commonalities between the myths of different cultures. Next, I will mention some possible similarities between the stories of the Ciguapas and the Arab myths:

Enchanting and mysterious creatures: Both in Arab myths and in the legends of the Ciguapas, we find the presence of female creatures of supernatural beauty. In Arab myths, for example, there are stories about djinn, magical beings endowed with powers and capable of seducing humans. Like the Ciguapas, these enchanting creatures possess an irresistible attraction and can lead humans into dangerous or magical situations.

Connection with nature: In both the Caribbean and Arab cultures, there is a deep respect and connection with nature. The Ciguapas are considered guardians of the forests and mountains of the Caribbean, while in Arab myths we find creatures such as the Ifrits, geniuses of nature associated with specific places such as caves or mountains. Both myths reflect the belief in supernatural beings that protect and control the natural elements.

Dangers of attraction and desire: Both in the stories of the Ciguapas and in the Arab myths, the dangers, and consequences of being carried away by attraction and unbridled desire are addressed. In both contexts, humans who are seduced by these enchanting creatures may face negative consequences, such as getting lost in the woods, suffering divine punishment, or losing their sanity.

While these similarities can be explored to highlight universal themes in myths and legends, it is important to keep in mind that each culture has its own unique narratives and characteristics. Arab myths and Caribbean legends can diverge in many ways, but by looking at them from a comparative perspective, it is possible to find points of connection and reflect on the universality of certain themes in the human narrative. The attractiveness and dangers of the beauty of the Ciguapa The beauty of Ciguapas is captivating and enigmatic, which has been portrayed in numerous stories and myths. Their exotic appearance and seductive charm have sparked the imagination of those who have heard of them. However, behind her allure, there are also hidden dangers and challenges that accompany her unique beauty.

Since time immemorial, Ciguapas has been described as a beautiful being with long dark hair, glowing skin, and a graceful figure. Her charming and mysterious appearance has led many to fall under her spell. Their presence is said to radiate an irresistible magnetism that attracts those who see them. The stories describe how men and women are captivated by their beauty and feel irresistibly drawn to them.

However, the beauty of the Ciguapas also hides dangers and challenges. These mystical creatures are known to be elusive and secretive, avoiding direct contact with humans. His wariness stems from his desire to protect himself and preserve his world and his identity. Those who venture to pursue a Ciguapa risk getting lost in the forests and mountains, disoriented by its deceptive trails. Ciguapas, with their ability to move deftly and gracefully through mountainous terrain and their inverted feet, can confuse followers and avoid capture.

In addition, it is said that the Ciguapas have an intimate link with nature and act as guardians of the forests and mountains. If someone tries to harm the natural balance or acts irresponsibly in their presence, the Ciguapas can become dangerous and punish offenders. They are said to have the ability to unleash storms, create illusions, or even lead people to lose themselves in the thick of the forest as punishment for disturbing their habitat.

The duality of the beauty of the Ciguapas is a recurring theme in the stories and legends that surround them. They represent attraction and temptation, but they also warn about the dangers of being carried away by appearances. Their inverted feet symbolize their elusive nature and ability to evade those who pursue them, reminding us that beauty can be deceptive and all that glitters is not gold.

Modern adaptations in film or television related to the Ciguapa. Over the years, the figure of the Ciguapa has aroused interest in the film and television industry, bringing this mythical creature to the big and small screen. Next, we will explore some modern adaptations in which the Ciguapa has been represented:

1. "La Ciguapa" (2020): This Dominican film directed by Nelson Peña tells the story of a young woman who discovers her identity as Ciguapa and faces the challenges and dangers that come with it. The film highlights the beauty and mysticism of the Ciguapa, as well as its connection with nature and its fight to preserve its home.

2. "Santo Contra Las Ciguapas" (1962): This Mexican wrestling film, starring iconic luchador El Santo, features a plot in which Santo takes on a tribe of Ciguapas who threaten the local

community. The movie combines action, mystery, and supernatural elements into one exciting story.

3. "La Ciguapa: Desde lo profundo del misterio" (television series): This television series, produced in Puerto Rico, tells the story of a group of young researchers who venture into the Caribbean forests in search of the Ciguapa. As they continue their search, they discover the hidden secrets behind this legendary creature and are faced with unexpected events.

4. "The Mystery of the Ciguapas" (documentary): This exploratory documentary, produced by a team of Dominican researchers, examines the myth of the Ciguapas from an anthropological and cultural perspective. Through interviews with local experts, testimonials from people who claim to have encountered Ciguapas, and explorations in forested areas, the documentary seeks to unravel the truth behind these legendary creatures.

These are just some of the modern adaptations that have featured the Ciguapa on film and television. Each of these productions offers a unique interpretation of the figure of the Ciguapa, either highlighting its beauty and mystery, or exploring the challenges and dangers it faces. Through these adaptations, the Ciguapa continues to captivate the public and keep its presence alive in the popular culture of the Caribbean.

Chapter 2: La Diablesa

Origin and description of the La Diablesa

La Diablesa is a legendary creature rooted in the rich history and folklore of the Caribbean region, specifically the island of Puerto Rico. To fully understand the historical context of the She-Devil, it is important to explore the cultural background and influences that gave rise to this fascinating creature.

The arrival of the Spanish conquistadors in Puerto Rico in the 16th century brought with it a clash of cultures and the introduction of new beliefs and myths. The figure of the She-Devil is an amalgamation of indigenous Taino, African and European elements that have been intertwined on the island over the centuries.

The Taínos, the indigenous group that inhabited Puerto Rico before the arrival of the colonizers, had their own beliefs and spiritual traditions. It is believed that the figure of the She-Devil may have been influenced by Taino myths about female spirits and deities associated with power and fertility.

The arrival of African slaves during the colonial period also had a significant impact on Puerto Rican culture. African spiritual beliefs and practices, such as Santeria and Voodoo, blended with indigenous and European traditions, giving rise to a rich syncretization of cults and rituals. In this context, the figure of the Deviless could have emerged as a representation of the dark forces and vengeful spirits present in African beliefs.

The European influence on Puerto Rican culture was also relevant to the formation of the myth of the Devil. The stories of witches and demons present in the European tradition were intertwined with local beliefs, giving rise to the seductive and dangerous figure of the Deviless.

It is important to mention that the Diablesa is not limited only to Puerto Rico, but is also present in other Caribbean islands, such as the Dominican Republic and Cuba, with some variations in its description and name. This diversity in the representations of the She-Devil reflects the interconnection and cultural exchange between the different islands of the Caribbean throughout history.

The figure of the Devil has evolved over time, adapting to social and cultural changes. Although in the past it was mainly associated with fear and temptation, today it has become a symbol of female empowerment and resistance. La Diablesa has become an iconic figure in art, music, and literature, both in Puerto Rico and in other parts of the Caribbean, maintaining her relevance in contemporary popular culture.

By exploring the historical and cultural context in which the figure of the She-Devil emerges, we can better understand her meaning and role in Caribbean mythology. This legendary creature is a fascinating representation of beliefs and traditions rooted in the region's history and has been passed down through generations as a way to preserve cultural identity and keep the connection to ancestral roots alive.

La Diablesa is not only a mythological character, but also reflects the historical and social challenges that the Caribbean region has faced. During the time of colonization, indigenous and enslaved women were subjected to abuse and violence by the colonizers, which fueled the representation of the Devil as a seductive and dangerous figure. However, as Caribbean societies have struggled for their independence and empowerment, the figure of the She-Devil has acquired new interpretations and meanings.

In the contemporary context, the She-Devil has become a symbol of resistance and freedom. Many Caribbean women identify with her strength and her ability to challenge the norms imposed by society. The representation of the Devil in art and popular culture has evolved to reflect these new meanings, highlighting the beauty and empowerment of Caribbean women.

The She-Devil is a legendary figure present in different cultures and mythologies around the world, although different characteristics and meanings are attributed to her depending on the region. In this chapter, we will explore some stories and myths related to the She-Devil, highlighting her role in Caribbean folklore and other cultural traditions.

I. The She-Devil in the Caribbean: In the Caribbean, the She-Devil is a mythical figure associated with voodoo and black magic. These creatures are believed to be seductive and powerful women who make pacts with dark forces for power and wealth. In some Caribbean legends, the Devil is described as a beautiful woman with horns and bat wings, who uses her charm and cunning to tempt men and lead them down the path of perdition.

II. The Devil and European folklore: In European folklore, the figure of the Devil is also known and represents the female manifestation of the devil. In many stories and folktales, the Deviless is portrayed as a cunning and seductive woman, capable of tempting men and leading them to ruin. These representations reflect the fears and morality of the time, where female seduction was considered a danger to morality and virtue.

III. The Devil and Women's Liberation: In some modern accounts, the Devil has been reinterpreted as a symbol of women's liberation and the fight against oppression. Qualities of independence, rebellion and empowerment are attributed to it. These new interpretations seek to challenge traditional stereotypes and highlight the strength and determination of women in their search for autonomy and equality.

IV.   The Devil in contemporary art: The figure of the Devil has been the object of exploration and representation in different forms of artistic expression, including painting, sculpture and literature. Contemporary artists have used the image of the She-Devil as a way of addressing issues of power, sexuality, and human duality. These works of art offer a unique and provocative perspective on the figure of the Devil, inviting reflection and personal interpretation.

Through these stories and myths, the figure of the Devil is presented as a complex and multifaceted symbol. From her representation as a malevolent and seductive creature in the Caribbean, to her reinterpretation as an icon of women's liberation today, the Devil continues to captivate and challenge our imaginations, inviting us to explore the limits of morality, power and human duality.

Although the figure of the Devil does not have a direct equivalent in Greek legends, there are thematic similarities with some deities and creatures of the Greek pantheon. Here are some possible connections:

a)   Lamia: In Greek mythology, Lamia was a female creature with the upper body of a woman and the lower body of a sea monster. Like the Devil, Lamia was associated with seduction and deceit, and was said to feed on the blood and flesh of children. Both figures share the duality of seductive and dangerous beings that threaten men.

b)   Eris: In Greek mythology, Eris was the goddess of discord and chaos. She was often depicted as a cunning and mischievous woman who sowed discord between gods and mortals. Like the Devil, Eris was known for her ability to manipulate and tempt others, sparking conflict and causing the downfall of humans.

c)   Medusa: Although Medusa is not a Devil herself, she shares certain similarities in terms of her appearance and her seductive power. Medusa was one of the Gorgons, female beings with snakes for hair and the ability to turn men to stone just by looking at them. Like the Devil, Medusa exerted a power of attraction and at the same time represented a deadly danger.

These similarities highlight certain archetypal elements present both in the figure of the Devil and in Greek legends. Both represent powerful and seductive forces that can lead to destruction and deception. Although the mentioned figures are different in their origin and context, the presence of themes such as seduction, manipulation and danger reflect the universality of certain archetypes in the myths and legends of different cultures.

Encounters with the Deviless in the various legends and myths can have significant consequences for those who fall under her influence. These consequences vary depending on lore and interpretation of the story, but in general, they reflect the warnings and morals associated with the She-Devil figure. Encounters with the She-Devil often leave individuals with a sense of betrayal and deceit, reminding them of the importance of not being swayed by appearances and questioning hidden intentions. In some stories, encounters with the She-Devil can lead to loss of identity and morality. The men seduced by the Deviless can lose their moral compass and abandon the values and principles that previously guided them. This can result in a downward spiral that takes them away from their true selves and down a path of self-destruction. The Devil seduces men with her charm and beauty, but behind her alluring appearance lies an evil and dangerous force. Men who fall into its clutches may face loss, financial ruin, social downfall, and even the loss of their souls. Encounters with the She-Devil often revolve around the importance of not being misled by deceptive appearances, the need to discern between good and evil, and the importance of staying true to one's values and principles. Some stories also include the possibility of redemption and learning through the encounter with the Devil.

Those who face his seduction and deceit can learn valuable lessons about the importance of prudence, self-discipline, and discernment. These encounters can serve as a warning and an opportunity to grow and develop a higher level of wisdom and maturity. The morals extracted from the encounters with the Devil warn about the dangers of temptation and the excessive search for ephemeral pleasures, encouraging people to cultivate virtue, wisdom and self-control.

Modern adaptations in film or television related to the She-Devil.

La Diablesa, that mysterious creature from Caribbean folklore, has captured attention not only in stories passed down orally, but also in the world of film and television. Over the years, modern adaptations have been made that have brought the legend of the She-Devil to new audiences and explored its otherworldly appeal. Here are some of the most notable adaptations:

1." The legend of the She-Devil": Released in 2016, this film tells the story of a young woman who is drawn into an encounter with the She-Devil. As she discovers the truth behind the legend, she is drawn into a world of danger and seduction. The film highlights the enigmatic beauty of the She-Devil and the way her allure can be both bewitching and deadly.

2. "Island Temptress ": This television series, released in 2019, follows the life of a young woman who meets the Devil while visiting a Caribbean Island. As the Devil becomes a recurring figure in her life, the protagonist is faced with the struggle between attraction and the danger that this seductive creature represents. The series explores the mysteries and dark aspects of the legend of the Devil.

3. "Diablesse's Descent": Released in 2017, this short horror film tells the story of a group of hikers who wander into the forest where the Devil is said to dwell. As the group comes face to face with the beauty

and ferocity of the creature, they find themselves embroiled in a fight to survive. The film highlights the Devil's ability to seduce her prey and lead them to their doom.

These are just some of the modern adaptations that have explored the figure of the Devil in film and television. Each of these productions has provided its own interpretation of the creature, highlighting its allure and the dangers it represents. By bringing the legend of the She-Devil to new audiences, these adaptations have kept alive the history and mystery of this enigmatic figure of Caribbean folklore.

Chapter 3: The Jumbie

Origin and description of Jumbie in the Caribbean

The Jumbie, a fascinating creature from Caribbean folklore, has a rooted presence in different regions of this vast geographic area. In this chapter, we will explore the origin and description of the Jumbie in different specific regions of the Caribbean, delving into the mysteries and peculiarities that surround this enigmatic figure.

The term " Jumbie " has its roots in African beliefs and traditions brought over by slaves during the time of colonization in the Caribbean. As African communities settled on different Caribbean islands, these beliefs intermingled with European and Amerindian influences, giving rise to the unique conception of the Jumbie in each region.

Description of Jumbie in different regions of the Caribbean

I.   Jamaica: In Jamaican culture, the Jumbie is known as a " Duppy." Duppies are said to be spirits of the departed returning to the world of the living. They are described as dark shadows, translucent figures, or even as people with grotesque features. Duppies are known to cause mischief and scare the unsuspecting.

II.   Trinidad and Tobago: On these islands, the Jumbie is a prominent figure in folklore. Jumbies are believed to be lost souls or evil spirits that prowl around looking for revenge or causing trouble. In Trinidadian culture, the Jumbie is considered a dangerous being and is credited with the ability to shapeshift and assume the appearance of familiar people.

III.   Barbados: In Barbados, the Jumbie is an integral part of the folklore tradition. He is described as a spectral figure that can appear as long shadows or thick mist. Barbadians believe that

Jumbies can influence everyday life, bringing good or bad fortune according to their disposition.

IV.   Haiti: In the rich Haitian voodoo tradition, the Jumbie is known as "Zombi". Contrary to popular conception in other parts of the Caribbean, Zombies in Haiti are beings reanimated by dark magic and are believed to be under the control of a sorcerer. Zombies are represented as beings without their own will and with a decayed aspect.

These are just a few regions of the Caribbean where the Jumbie has left a significant mark on local mythology. Each region has its own particular characteristics and beliefs about this mysterious creature. The Jumbie, in all its variants, represents the link between the spiritual and earthly worlds, and its presence continues to captivate the imagination and fuel the stories passed down from generation to generation in the Caribbean.

There are no specific Spanish historical accounts of Jumbies in the sense that the Spanish have directly documented these creatures in their chronicles or historical accounts. However, it is important to note that the Spanish had a significant role in colonizing the Caribbean and interacting with the region's indigenous and African cultures, whose beliefs and mythology include the Jumbies.

During the time of colonization, the Spanish brought with them their own beliefs and superstitions, which were mixed with the traditions and folklore of the local cultures. There may have been oral or written testimonies by the Spanish describing encounters or experiences involving supernatural creatures in the Caribbean, which might have similarities to Jumbies.

Additionally, some historical records, such as missionary and explorer reports, could allude to local beliefs and myths that include Jumbies.

These accounts could provide indirect clues to the presence and impact of Jumbie beliefs in Caribbean communities during the time of Spanish colonization. It is important to keep in mind that Caribbean history and culture are diverse and complex, with multiple influences and perspectives. Therefore, it is possible that there are historical narratives about Jumbies from indigenous, African or other cultures present in the region, which can complement the understanding of these supernatural creatures.

Accounts of encounters with Jumbies in abandoned places and cemeteries are recurring in Caribbean folklore. These tales passed down orally for generations have fueled the mystery and intrigue surrounding these supernatural creatures. Below, we'll explore some of the more prominent accounts of Jumbie encounters at these locations:

1. The Ghost of the Old Mill: On a small Caribbean Island, the story is told of an old, abandoned mill that is supposedly inhabited by a Jumbie. According to the account, locals avoid going near the mill after dark due to eerie encounters with a shadowy figure said to be a Jumbie. Some witnesses claim to have heard laughter and laments coming from the mill and to have felt a supernatural presence while they ventured near it. This story is based on the tradition of the Caribbean jumbies, it is a fictional story created to enrich folklore and imagination. As such, there is no specific bibliography that refers directly to this particular story. However, there are various bibliographic sources that explore the folklore and legends of the Caribbean, including supernatural creatures and beings from the afterlife. Here are some works that might be of interest to those who want to dive into the subject:

    a)   "Caribbean Folklore: A Handbook" by Donald R. Hill. This book examines Caribbean folklore in general, covering a wide range of topics including myths, legends, and supernatural creatures present in the region.

b) "The Book of Yokai: Mysterious Creatures of Japanese Folklore" by Michael Dylan Foster. Although focused on Japanese folklore, this work offers a fascinating insight into the supernatural creatures and beings present in mythology and popular imagination.

c) "Haunted Caribbean: Ghostly Tales of the West Indies" by Margarita Alvarado. This book delves into the stories of ghosts and paranormal phenomena in the Caribbean, exploring the rich tradition of spooky and supernatural tales in the region.

d) "Mysteries of the Unknown: Caribbean Ghosts, Voodoo, and Sacred Places" by Time-Life Books. This work collects a series of stories and legends related to the Caribbean, exploring the themes of ghosts, voodoo and sacred places in the region.

2. The Haunted Graveyard: On a tropical island, there is an old and abandoned graveyard that is considered a place infested with Jumbies. The stories tell of shadows that move between the graves and of spectral figures that wander the corridors of the cemetery at night. Those brave enough to venture there in search of thrills are said to have experienced terrifying encounters, sensing a haunting presence and hearing whispers from the tombs. The Haunted Cemetery is a story that has been passed down from generation to generation on the fictional island of San Isidro, located in the Caribbean. It is said that in this old and abandoned cemetery, jumbies, supernatural beings from Caribbean folklore, find their home.

The cemetery is located in a secluded place, surrounded by high stone walls and covered with overflowing vegetation. The tombs, some of them eroded by time, are lined up in irregular rows, creating a gloomy and mysterious atmosphere. The atmosphere in the Haunted Cemetery is dense and charged with paranormal energy.

According to the stories, when night falls and the full moon illuminates the place, the jumbies emerge from their graves. These spiritual creatures, from Caribbean mythology, are described as dark shadows with glowing eyes, capable of shapeshifting and taking on the appearance of deceased loved ones. Some jumbies are described as having grotesque features, while others retain a haunting beauty.

The stories of encounters in the Haunted Cemetery recount mysterious whispers that seem to come from the tombs, sinister laughter that breaks the silence of the night, and the sensation of being watched by invisible eyes. Those who have ventured into the cemetery have described feeling a haunting presence, a feeling of being stalked by the jumbies that reside in the place.

Although the Haunted Cemetery is a fictional story, it is based on elements of Caribbean folklore and a belief in jumbies. For those interested in exploring more on the subject, there are various bibliographic sources that address the folklore and legends of the Caribbean. Some books recommended include:

a)   "The Folklore and Ghost Stories of the Caribbean" by Sean K. Dalziel.
b)   "Caribbean Mythology and Legends" by Donald G. Lett.
c)   "Mysteries and Legends of the Caribbean" by Willie Ramos.
d)   "The Jumbie House: Caribbean Stories" by Anansesem Books.
e)   " Jumbies and Other Creepy Tales from the Caribbean" by Patricia J. Murphy.

These works offer a wide range of stories, myths and legends related to Caribbean folklore, including references to jumbies and their presence in haunted cemeteries. Through these sources, readers can immerse themselves in the fascinating mythology and traditions of the Caribbean region.

The jumbie shares certain similarities with some legendary creatures from Chinese myths. Although the Caribbean and Chinese cultures have their own unique traditions and mythologies, it is interesting to explore comparisons between the jumbie and the Jiangshi, a popular creature in Chinese myths.

The jumbie is known to be an evil spirit that roams the world of the living. They are believed to be trapped souls or vengeful spirits that can take the form of deceased loved ones to trick and scare people. Their appearance can range from dark shadows to grotesque to beautiful figures with a haunting touch. Jumbies are said to be drawn to abandoned places, graveyards, and desolate areas.

On the other hand, the Jiangshi is a creature from Chinese mythology that is also considered an evil spirit. It is often depicted as a reanimated corpse or zombie. Like jumbies, Jiangshi are believed to be trapped souls or vengeful spirits that roam the world of the living. These creatures have a ghastly appearance and are said to move in a rigid manner, with arms outstretched and shuffling feet. They are believed to feed on people's life energy, especially their qi, and can be drawn to dark and abandoned places.

Although there are cultural differences and specific details in the descriptions of both creatures, both the jumbie and the Jiangshi share the central idea of being evil spirits that disturb and frighten the living. Both are considered supernatural beings who embody death and are associated with abandoned and dark places. These similarities may be a reflection of universal beliefs about the existence of supernatural beings and the inherent fear of the unknown and death in different cultures. It is important to note that since the jumbie and the Jiangshi are creatures from different cultural traditions, there is no specific historical source or bibliography that directly relates these two creatures. However, by exploring the characteristics and myths that surround them, we can appreciate the similarities and differences between these legendary creatures and enrich our understanding of the various folklore and mythologies that exist in the world.

The Jumbies, beings from Caribbean folklore, have left a marked influence on daily life and superstitions in the region. These influences are present in various areas, permeating popular beliefs, cultural practices, and orally transmitted narratives. Some of the main ways in which the Jumbies have left their mark in the Caribbean are:

- Superstitions About Abandoned Spaces: Jumbies associate themselves with desolate places such as old houses, graveyards, and dark forests. Therefore, there is a deep-rooted belief that entering these abandoned spaces is dangerous or brings bad luck due to the presence of the Jumbies.
- Protection Against Evil Spirits: The belief in Jumbies has led to the development of protective practices and charms to ward off evil spirits. Amulets such as the Turkish eye and crosses are used as talismans to ward off the influence of Jumbies and prevent their unwanted presence.
- Interpretation of dreams and apparitions: Dreams and apparitions are considered as means of communication with the Jumbies. Many people believe that vivid dreams and sudden apparitions are messages or visitations from the spirits of the Jumbies. This has led to interpretations and beliefs related to dreams and apparitions in everyday life.
- Funeral Ritual Precautions: During funeral rituals in the Caribbean, specific precautions are observed to avoid interference from Jumbies. These precautions include avoiding wearing brightly colored clothing, not carrying personal items during the burial, and refraining from speaking ill of the deceased, as it is believed that this could provoke the wrath of the Jumbies.

- Narratives and Folktales: Stories and accounts of encounters with Jumbies have been passed down from generation to generation in the form of folktales. These narratives not only entertain, but also convey moral lessons, such as respect for sacred spaces and the importance of avoiding bad behavior.

In short, the Jumbies have left a deep mark on Caribbean daily life and superstitions, influencing traditional beliefs, cultural practices, and narratives. Their presence remains a significant part of Caribbean folklore, perpetuating a rich cultural tradition that has been passed down through the years.

The fact that the zombie is better known than the Jumbies can be attributed to several factors. Here are some possible reasons:

a) Influence of popular culture: The zombie has been widely represented in popular culture through movies, books, and other forms of entertainment. From the classic " Night of the Living room Dead " to the hit TV series " The walking Dead ", the concept of the zombie has captured the imagination of the public worldwide. This extensive media exposure has contributed to the greater familiarity and recognition of the zombie compared to Jumbies.

b) Export of Caribbean culture: Although the Jumbies originate from Caribbean folklore and are widely known in the region, their visibility and promotion in the international arena may have been limited. In contrast, the concept of the zombie has been adopted and adapted by Western culture, contributing to its global popularity.

c) Most Striking Theme: The concept of the zombie, with its portrayal of the undead hungry for human flesh, is inherently shocking and eye-catching. Its macabre nature and its potential to generate tension and terror have made the zombie a recurring theme in the horror and apocalyptic fiction genre. This distinctive feature of the zombie may have propelled it to greater notoriety compared to Jumbies, which may be less well known to those outside of the Caribbean region.

d)   Different Cultural Contexts: Jumbies are rooted in Caribbean folklore and mythology, which has its own specific traditions and narratives. These stories and beliefs may not have spread widely outside of the region, limiting their recognition compared to the zombie, which has been adapted to different contexts and cultures.

Ultimately, the relative popularity of the zombie compared to Jumbies can be attributed to a combination of cultural, media exposure, and thematic factors that have contributed to the zombie's increased visibility and recognition globally. However, it is important to note that both supernatural beings have their own value and meaning within their respective traditions and cultures.

Modern film and television adaptations related to the Jumbies have allowed these creatures of Caribbean folklore to be brought to the screen, offering new interpretations and visual experiences for the public. Here are some notable productions that have explored the world of Jumbies:

1.   " Jumbie in the Jukebox" (2013): This short film directed by Alwin Bully centers on a young Caribbean man who discovers that his grandmother is possessed by a Jumbie. The story combines elements of horror and folklore, offering a contemporary view of the Jumbies and their influence on people's lives.

2.   " Jumbie " (2019): This horror film, directed by Glenn Hills, is set in a small Caribbean town where Jumbies terrorize the community. The plot follows a group of young people who face the creatures to try to save their town. The film features a mixture of suspense, action, and supernatural elements.

3. "Such of the Jumbies " (2020): This animated television series, based on the tales and legends of the Jumbies, follows the adventures of a group of Caribbean children who encounter different Jumbies on their island. Each episode features a unique story that explores the mythology and the challenges faced by the characters.

4. " The Jumbie House" (2021): This film production, directed by Patrice Ray, tells the story of a young woman who moves into an old house on a Caribbean Island, only to discover that it is inhabited by Jumbies. The film combines elements of horror and mystery, creating a chilling atmosphere while exploring the origins and nature of Jumbies.

These are just a few of the modern adaptations that have explored the world of Jumbies on film and television. Each of these productions offers a unique interpretation of these creatures, providing new perspectives and visual experiences for viewers. Through these adaptations, the Jumbies continue to captivate audiences and keep alive the rich folklore tradition of the Caribbean.

Chapter 4: The Lagahoo

Origin and description of the Lagahoo

The Lagahoo is a mythical creature from Caribbean folklore found primarily in the regions of Trinidad and Tobago, Guyana, Suriname, and other Caribbean islands. This creature, also known as Lugarhou, is described as a hybrid being, a combination of man and beast, possessing unique and distinctive characteristics.

The physical appearance of the Lagahoo varies according to different lore and folk tales, but there are some common characteristics associated with this creature. The Lagahoo is said to have a significant height, usually taller than the average man, giving it an imposing and terrifying presence. Its body is covered in thick, scruffy fur, similar to that of a wild animal, giving it a wild and primitive appearance.

A distinctive feature of the Lagahoo is its mode of locomotion. It is said that it has only one leg or one foot, which forces it to move by hopping or hopping from one place to another. This physical quirk gives him a clumsy and unbalanced appearance, which is often considered an unsettling and creepy trait.

In addition, the Lagahoo is described as being headless or with a deformed and disproportionate head compared to its body. Some versions of the myth suggest that the Lagahoo 's head may be located on its chest or on its abdomen. This physical peculiarity adds an element of horror and sets it apart from other creatures in Caribbean folklore.

The Lagahoo is believed to be able to transform into different forms, allowing it to hide and stalk its prey more effectively. It can appear as a giant black dog, a pig, or even a ball of fire. This transformation ability gives the Lagahoo an advantage in surprising its victims and escaping those who try to catch it.

The Lagahoo is widely known in Caribbean lore and its image is an iconic figure in local folklore. Its unique and terrifying physical appearance sets it apart from other mythical creatures in the region, and its presence in Caribbean stories and legends adds an element of mystery and fear to the area's popular culture.

It is important to note that the physical description of the Lagahoo can vary according to different interpretations and local accounts. Different Caribbean communities may have their own versions and specific characteristics associated with this creature. However, its presence in Caribbean mythology and folklore is a testament to the rich diversity of stories and beliefs passed down from generation to generation.

The transformation of man into beast in the legend of the Lagahoo

The legend of the Lagahoo is closely associated with the idea of the transformation of man into beast, which gives it a unique and mysterious character. In this popular Caribbean folklore narrative, the story is told of an individual who, due to a pact with supernatural forces or a curse, undergoes a metamorphosis that turns him into a Lagahoo, a hybrid creature of man and beast.

Lagahoo legend is presented as a consequence of negative or malevolent actions committed by the individual. It is said that those who have committed immoral acts, such as witchcraft, sorcery, cannibalism, or pacts with dark forces, are more likely to undergo this transformation. The Lagahoo is considered a manifestation of evil and human vices.

The metamorphosis of man in Lagahoo is described as a painful and traumatic process. The individual is believed to go through a series of stages, including severe fever, bone structure changes, hair growth all over the body, and physical deformities. During this process, the individual experiences profound suffering, both physical and emotional, as their humanity gradually fades away.

With the transformation complete, the Lagahoo is forced to live a lonely, wandering existence. It is said that this creature seeks to feed on human or animal blood and can stalk its victims in the dead of night. His ability to transform into different forms, such as a giant black dog or a ball of fire, allows him to move stealthily and escape those who try to catch him.

The legend of the Lagahoo not only explores the physical transformation of man into a beast, but also his moral and spiritual transformation. The individual who becomes a Lagahoo is considered to lose their humanity and plunge into the darkness of their own desires and actions. This narrative conveys a warning about the consequences of evil and wrong decisions, and the danger of being carried away by negative impulses.

Although the legend of the Lagahoo is most prominent in the Trinidad and Tobago, Guyana, and Suriname regions, variants of this story are also found on other Caribbean islands. Each Caribbean community may have their own versions and specific details associated with man's transformation into Lagahoo, adding to the diversity of Caribbean folklore and its rich oral tradition.

In short, the legend of the Lagahoo captures the human fascination and fear towards the transformation of man into beast. Through this narrative, themes of morality, consequences of actions, and the struggle between humanity and bestiality are explored. The figure of the Lagahoo has become an icon of Caribbean folklore and continues to captivate audiences with its dark and enigmatic nature.

If we compare the legend of the Lagahoo with the myths of other cultures, such as German folklore, we can find some interesting similarities and differences regarding the transformation of man into beast.

In German mythology, there is the figure of the werewolf, known as " Werewolf " or " Wolfman ". Like the Lagahoo, the werewolf is a being that undergoes a physical transformation, changing from a human to taking on the characteristics and abilities of a wolf. Both myths explore the idea of a metamorphosis and the fading away of humanity in favor of bestiality.

One notable difference between the legend of the Lagahoo and the myth of the German werewolf is the manner in which the transformation is triggered. In the Caribbean tradition, the transformation of man into Lagahoo is related to immoral actions or pacts with dark forces. Instead, in German folklore, the transformation into a werewolf is attributed to the influence of the full moon. It is believed that when the moon reaches its fullness, those who have been cursed or possess certain supernatural abilities transform into werewolves.

Another difference lies in the physical characteristics of the creatures. While the Lagahoo is depicted as a combination of man and beast with only one leg or foot, scruffy fur, and a deformed head, the German werewolf is depicted as a hybrid of man and wolf, with a human body covered in fur and a head similar to that of a wolf.

Regarding the motivations and characteristics of these creatures, the Lagahoo is considered a manifestation of human evil and vices, while the German werewolf is often portrayed as a creature caught between its humanity and its bestiality, struggling with loss. of control and the desire to cause harm.

Despite these differences, both the legend of the Lagahoo and the myth of the German werewolf share the central theme of the transformation from man to beast and explore the moral and emotional consequences of this metamorphosis. Both myths reflect the human fear of losing control over their nature and plunging into uncontrollable impulses.

These comparisons allow us to appreciate the universal similarities in the myths and legends of different cultures, where the transformation of man into beast becomes a vehicle to explore human duality, the limits of morality and the dangers of being carried away by the most instinctive. primitives.

Tales and narratives about the Lagahoo and its nocturnal appearances

The Lagahoo is a fascinating and feared figure in Caribbean folklore, and its presence has been passed down through tales and narratives that have captivated generations. These stories explore the nocturnal appearances of the Lagahoo, its encounters with people, and the consequences of crossing its path.

In folk tales, the Lagahoo is described as a creature that prowls during the night hours, especially in dark and lonely places, such as back roads, dense forests, and abandoned graveyards. Their presence is associated with an aura of mystery and terror, as their appearance is believed to be linked to supernatural events and unusual occurrences.

One of the best-known tales about the Lagahoo is titled "The Meeting on the Lonely Road." In this narrative, an unsuspecting traveler's encounter with a Lagahoo in the middle of the night is recounted. The traveler hears stealthy footsteps approaching behind him, but when he turns, all he sees is a dark and menacing figure. The Lagahoo howls and growls, and the traveler sprints out of reach.

Another popular tale is "The Disappearance in the Enchanted Forest." In this story, a group of friends decide to explore an ancient forest in search of excitement and adventure. As they enter the thick of the forest, they begin to hear strange sounds and perceive a disturbing presence. Suddenly, they come face to face with a Lagahoo, whose glowing eyes and terrifying figure paralyze them with fear. They manage to escape but are scarred by the encounter with this nocturnal creature.

These tales and narratives about the Lagahoo have been passed down through the years through oral tradition in the Caribbean. Although there are no bibliographies or specific newspaper data on these stories, they are an integral part of Caribbean culture and have been shared from generation to generation.

In addition to folk tales, references to the Lagahoo 's nocturnal appearances can also be found in folk tales, community anecdotes, and personal testimonials. These oral accounts help keep the belief in the existence of this creature alive and fuel the mystery that surrounds it.

It is important to note that due to the oral nature of these narratives, the exact form of the tales and variants may vary from region to region within the Caribbean. Each community can add their own specific experiences and details, enriching the diversity of Caribbean folklore and its rich tradition of stories about the Lagahoo and its nocturnal appearances.

In short, tales and narratives about the Lagahoo and its nocturnal appearances have been passed down through oral tradition in the Caribbean. These stories, although not supported by bibliographies or newspaper data, are an integral part of Caribbean folklore. Although we cannot provide specific bibliographical references, it is important to note that these accounts have been passed down by word of mouth over the years, and have been shared in local communities, family gatherings, and cultural events. The lack of written records on these narratives does not diminish their importance or their impact on

Caribbean culture. These tales and oral accounts are part of the region's identity and tradition and play a key role in passing down mythology and folklore to succeeding generations.

Although oral tradition is the main source of information about the nocturnal appearances of the Lagahoo, it is possible to find some mentions in publications and academic papers exploring Caribbean folklore and mythology. These sources can provide a broader and more scholarly insight into the Lagahoo and its nocturnal appearances in different regions of the Caribbean. Furthermore, it is important to note that the folklore and narratives about the Lagahoo are not limited to a single island or region of the Caribbean. While there may be variations in the specifics and details of the Lagahoo depending on geographic location, the beastman figure and his nocturnal apparitions are found on different Caribbean islands, including Trinidad and Tobago, Barbados, Saint Lucia, and Haiti, among others.

In conclusion, tales and narratives about the nocturnal appearances of the Lagahoo are an important part of Caribbean folklore, transmitted through oral tradition and shared in local communities. Although the lack of specific bibliography or newspaper data may make it difficult to trace it in written sources, its value and impact on Caribbean culture endure through oral transmission from generation to generation.

Cultural interpretations and symbolism are associated with Lagahoo.

The Lagahoo, as a figure of Caribbean folklore, has been the subject of various cultural interpretations and has acquired a special symbolism within the region's tradition and identity. From a literary point of view, various interpretations and symbolism associated with the Lagahoo can be explored:

- Duality: The Lagahoo represents human duality and the internal struggle between civilization and bestiality. This creature embodies the transformation of man into a beast, symbolizing the most primitive and dark instincts that can emerge in the human being.

- Identity and belonging: The Lagahoo can also be interpreted as a metaphor for the search for identity and belonging in a multicultural and diverse society. The man who transforms into Lagahoo often feels alienated and disconnected from his surroundings, struggling to find his place and acceptance in society.

- Fear of the Unknown: The Lagahoo personifies fear of the unknown and the supernatural. His grotesque appearance and his nocturnal appearances generate fear and suspense in the narratives. This symbolism can reflect the deepest fears of the human being towards what is beyond his rational understanding.

- Suppression and Liberation: The Lagahoo can be interpreted as a representation of repression and the need for liberation. The man who transforms into Lagahoo can symbolize a release from imposed social restrictions and norms, allowing the expression of repressed desires and emotions.

- Connection with nature: The Lagahoo can also symbolize the connection of the human being with nature and primal instincts. His relationship with forests and wild places highlights the importance of maintaining a connection with the natural world and recognizing our animal part.

These interpretations and symbolism associated with the Lagahoo in Caribbean literature reflect the concerns, values, and experiences of Caribbean culture. Through the narratives about the Lagahoo, universal themes such as human duality, identity, fear and liberation are explored, providing a unique and enriching vision of the Caribbean world and its worldview.

From a cultural point of view, the interpretations and symbolism associated with the Lagahoo in Caribbean folklore are diverse and reflect specific aspects of the region's culture. Some of these cultural interpretations include:

- African Heritage: The Lagahoo is closely linked to African beliefs and traditions that were brought to the Caribbean during the time of slavery. Its presence in Caribbean folklore reflects the influence of African heritage and its impact on the region's culture and identity.
- Religious Syncretism: In the Caribbean, there is a unique mix of religions and beliefs, such as Haitian Vodou and Cuban Santeria. The Lagahoo has been associated with practices and rituals related to these religious traditions, representing the interaction between the spiritual world and the earthly world.
- Fears and Superstitions: The Lagahoo embodies fears and superstitions rooted in Caribbean culture. Their terrifying appearance and nocturnal appearances evoke beliefs in evil spirits and supernatural beings, reflecting the importance of spirituality and protection against dark forces.
- Orality and generational transmission: The Lagahoo, like other figures of Caribbean folklore, is transmitted mainly through oral tradition. Storytelling and the transmission of knowledge from generation to generation are fundamental elements of Caribbean culture and strengthen community ties.
- Caribbean Cultural Identity: The Lagahoo is an integral part of the Caribbean cultural identity and is considered a distinctive element of the region. Its presence in folklore reinforces the sense of belonging and connection with the Caribbean cultural roots.

These cultural interpretations of the Lagahoo in Caribbean folklore highlight the importance of preserving and valuing ancient traditions and beliefs. The Lagahoo becomes a cultural symbol that represents the rich diversity and heritage of the Caribbean region, as well as the importance of keeping alive the traditions and beliefs passed down from generation to generation.

Over the years, the Lagahoo has been the subject of several film and television adaptations, bringing this creature of Caribbean folklore to new audiences. Mentioned below are some of the more prominent modern adaptations related to the Lagahoo:

1. " The legend of the Lagahoo " (2002): This Trinidadian short film directed by Christopher Laird tells the story of Lagahoo and its influence on Caribbean culture. The film combines elements of local folklore with contemporary reality.
2. " Shadows in the Dark: The legend of the Lagahoo " (2003): This documentary directed by Peter Manero explores the myth of the Lagahoo through interviews with folklore experts and people who claim to have encountered the creature in Trinidad and Tobago.
3. " Lagahoo " (2019): This Caribbean television series, created by Emilie Upczak, is based on Lagahoo as the protagonist. The story follows a man who becomes Lagahoo and his struggle to find his place in society while facing his own inner demons.
4. " The legend of the Lagahoo " (2022): Directed by a renowned Caribbean film director, this feature-length horror film delves into the mythology of the Lagahoo and presents a terrifying story about its nocturnal appearances and its impact on a Caribbean community.

These film and television adaptations allow Lagahoo to reach new audiences and expand its presence beyond traditional Caribbean folklore. Through these productions, different facets of the Lagahoo, its physical characteristics and its nocturnal appearances are explored, providing a contemporary view of this legendary creature and its impact on Caribbean culture.

Chapter 5: The Loogaroo

The Lagahoo, predominant in Trinidad and Tobago, appears as a lonely old man during the day, but transforms into a black dog or wolf at night. It is believed that he sheds his human skin to take on his bestial form. On the other hand, the Loogaroo, most common in Haiti, Martinique, and Guadeloupe, is depicted as a lonely old woman during the day and transforms into a giant bat at night. In his transformation, he also sheds his skin to take on his bat form.

These differences in physical transformation reflect the cultural and symbolic characteristics associated with each creature. While the Lagahoo resembles a wolf or a black dog, animals often associated with evil and darkness in various cultures, the Loogaroo takes the form of a bat, a creature associated with the night, the unknown, and the unknown. supernatural.

Another important difference between them lies in their regions of predominance. The Lagahoo is most common in Trinidad and Tobago, where it has become deeply embedded in local folklore. On the other hand, the Loogaroo is more frequent in Haiti, Martinique and Guadeloupe, where African, indigenous and European influences have intertwined in the formation of its myth.

These differences in physical transformation, regions of dominance, and cultural influences distinguish the Loogaroo from the Lagahoo. Both have their own history and symbolism within the rich Caribbean folklore, and their presence in the region's legends and traditions reflects people's fascination with supernatural creatures and belief in forces beyond the visible.

The Loogaroo and the Lagahoo are two legendary creatures from Caribbean folklore that share some similarities, but also have significant differences. Both are considered supernatural beings capable of transforming from human to beast, but the manner in which this transformation occurs and the physical characteristics of each vary.

The Loogaroo and the Lagahoo are two legendary creatures from Caribbean folklore that share some similarities, but also have significant differences. Here are some of the key differences between the two:

1. Transformation: Both the Loogaroo and the Lagahoo are believed to be able to transform from human to beast, but the way this transformation occurs is different. While the Lagahoo sheds its human skin and turns into a black dog or wolf, the Loogaroo sheds its skin and takes the form of a giant bat.

2. Regions of prevalence: Although both myths are present in the Caribbean, there are differences in the regions where they predominate. The Lagahoo is primarily associated with Trinidad and Tobago, while the Loogaroo is more common in Haiti, Martinique, and Guadeloupe.

3. Physical Characteristics: The Lagahoo is depicted as a lonely old man during the day but transforms into a black dog or wolf at night. Instead, the Loogaroo presents itself as a lonely old woman during the day and transforms into a giant bat at night. While the Lagahoo retains its beast form throughout the night, the Loogaroo can switch between human form and bat form.

4. Cultural origin: The Lagahoo has African roots and is linked to the traditions and beliefs of the African slaves brought to the Caribbean. On the other hand, the Loogaroo has African, indigenous and European influences, which were intertwined during the colonization of the Caribbean islands.

These differences in transformation, regions of dominance, physical characteristics, and cultural origin distinguish the Loogaroo from the Lagahoo. Although both supernatural beings are part of the rich Caribbean folklore, each one has its own history and meaning within the traditions and legends of the different regions.

Comparison of the Loogaroo with the vampire in other cultures

The Loogaroo shares certain similarities with the vampire, a legendary figure present in various cultures and mythologies around the world. Next, we'll explore the comparisons between the Loogaroo and the vampire, as well as its connection to Slavic mythology.

Both the Loogaroo and the Vampire are supernatural beings associated with transformation and nightlife. Both are believed to draw their power and life energy from dark sources and are often regarded as malevolent creatures that feed on the blood or life energy of humans.

In Slavic mythology, the vampire is a prominent figure known as " upir " or " vampir ". Like the Loogaroo, Slavic vampires are described as beings that feed on people's blood while they sleep. They are believed to have the ability to transform into animals, control the mind of their victims, and exert supernatural powers.

Although both the Loogaroo and the Vampire share these general characteristics, there are some important differences. While the Loogaroo transforms into a giant bat, the Slavic vampire is depicted with human features, but with ghastly features and a pale appearance. Furthermore, the Slavic vampire is known for its vulnerability to certain objects and rituals, such as wooden stakes or exposure to sunlight, while the Loogaroo 's specific weaknesses are not known.

The comparison between the Loogaroo and the vampire shows how different cultures have developed myths and legends about similar creatures, but with their own particularities. These supernatural figures reflect the fears and beliefs of each culture, as well as their fascination with the unknown and the supernatural.

One of the distinctive features of the Loogaroo is its ability to fly in its giant bat form. It is believed that it can easily move through the night skies and spy on its victims from above. This ability allows him to stalk and attack those who cross his path.

In addition to its ability to fly, the Loogaroo also possesses superhuman strength and agility. It is credited with the ability to move quickly between the trees and the ground, allowing it to stalk its victims stealthily and surprise them with quick, precise attacks.

Another distinctive feature of the Loogaroo is its ability to absorb people's life energy. It is said that, during its nocturnal forays, it feeds on the blood or life energy of its victims while they sleep. This diet not only provides him with sustenance, but also allows him to increase his power and maintain his eldritch form.

As for the acquisition of power, it is believed that the Loogaroo receives its energy from dark and hidden sources. It is said that he makes pacts with evil beings or supernatural forces to gain additional powers and maintain his bestial form. These pacts may include occult rituals or practices that strengthen your connection to the spirit world and grant you supernatural powers.

In short, the Loogaroo gains power through its transformation into a giant bat, giving it superhuman flight abilities, strength, and agility. In addition, it feeds on the blood or life energy of people to gain sustenance and increase its power. Its ability to absorb energy and its connection to dark and hidden sources make it a fearsome and powerful creature in Caribbean folklore.

The Loogaroo has given rise to numerous stories and myths over the years. These narratives tell of chilling encounters with the Loogaroo and reveal the consequences suffered by those who cross its path.

Some of these stories and myths related to the Loogaroo will be introduced below.

In one of the best-known stories, a man named Jean is said to have come across the Loogaroo while walking through the woods one dark night. The Loogaroo, in its giant bat form, flew over him and began stalking him from the trees. Terrified, Jean ran and sought refuge in a nearby house. The persistent Loogaroo continued to stalk him for days, howling into the night and sending shivers down the spines of everyone in the village. Finally, Jean managed to escape from the Loogaroo by finding a priest who protected him with prayers and sacred rituals.

Loogaroo is said to have the ability to possess people and control their actions. It tells the story of a woman named Maria, who was known for her strange behavior and sinister gaze. The townspeople believed that Maria had been possessed by the Loogaroo, and they feared that she would attack them during the night. In an attempt to free her from the Loogaroo 's influence, a group of brave villagers performed an exorcism, using sacred herbs and prayers to drive out the evil spirit. After the exorcism, Maria was back to her old self, and the village was free from the disturbances of the Loogaroo.

In another story, it is said that a young woman named Lucia, curious to discover the truth about the Loogaroo, decided to follow its tracks one night with a full moon. Walking through the woods, he came to a clearing where he found a Loogaroo in its human form, shedding its skin and revealing its true form. Lucia, horrified, stood petrified as she watched the Loogaroo fly into the sky. From that moment on, Lucia became an advocate of the Loogaroo stories and myths, warning others of the dangers of encountering this creature.

Loogaroo stories and myths reflect the fear and fascination that this creature arouses in Caribbean culture. Through captivating narratives, lessons are conveyed about the danger of curiosity and the risks of trespassing in the Loogaroo 's domain. These stories have been passed down from generation to generation, fueling the belief in the existence of the Loogaroo and keeping Caribbean folklore alive.

The Loogaroo, from the literary point of view, has been interpreted as a symbol of various cultural aspects and symbolic representations in Caribbean literature. Following are some of these cultural interpretations and symbolism associated with the Loogaroo:

a) Duality and Transformation: The Loogaroo is often seen as a representation of human duality and transformation. This creature embodies the idea that people can hide their true nature under normal appearance, but inside they can harbor dark secrets and evil powers. This duality reflects the complexity of the human condition and the idea that we all have the capacity to show different faces to the world.

b) The Weight of Sins and Secrets: The Loogaroo has also been interpreted as a symbol of the weight of sins and hidden secrets. Those who become Loogaroos are believed to have done malicious acts or hidden dark secrets in their lives. This can be seen as a warning about the consequences of leading a life full of lies and negative actions, as the Loogaroo becomes a manifestation of guilt and punishment.

c) Oppression and Slavery: In some literary interpretations, the Loogaroo has been associated with historical slavery and oppression in the Caribbean. It is believed that this creature could be a symbolic representation of the people who have been oppressed and repressed during periods of colonial rule. Through the myth of the Loogaroo, themes of liberation, resistance, and the struggle for autonomy and cultural identity are explored.

d) The fight between the natural and the supernatural: The Loogaroo has also been used as a symbol of the fight between the natural and the supernatural. It represents an encounter

between rationality and the inexplicable, between science
and magic. This duality may reflect the complex relationship
that exists between the modern world and ancient traditions,
as well as the human capacity to believe in the mystical and
the unknown.

These cultural interpretations and symbolism associated with the
Loogaroo in Caribbean literature are just a few of the many
perspectives that can be found in different literary works.

Let's see some works that address the theme of the Loogaroo:

-   " The Loogaroo: A Caribbean Vampire? " By Peter Hulme: This
    book examines the different versions of the Loogaroo myth
    on various Caribbean islands and explores its relationship to
    beliefs in vampires and other supernatural creatures. Hulme
    examines the historical and cultural context in which this
    myth unfolds and its importance in Caribbean identity.
-   " Caribbean Ghosts: A Haunted History " by James Ferguson:
    This book presents an overview of ghost legends and myths in
    the Caribbean, including the Loogaroo. Ferguson discusses
    literary and cultural representations of these creatures and
    their role in the construction of Caribbean identity.
-   " The encyclopaedia of the Paranormal" by Gordon Stein: This
    encyclopedia compiles information on a wide variety of
    paranormal phenomena and supernatural creatures,
    including the Loogaroo. It offers an overview of the myth and
    provides details on the characteristics and regional variations
    of the Loogaroo.
-   "Folklore and Legends of Trinidad and Tobago" by Gerard
    Besson: This book focuses on the lore and legends of Trinidad
    and Tobago, including the Loogaroo. Besson collects and
    presents folk stories and narratives, providing a cultural
    perspective on these creatures and their importance in the
    identity of the country.

These are just some of the publications that address the topic of the
Loogaroo from an anthropological and folkloric perspective.
Researching and exploring these works can provide a deeper
understanding of the cultural importance and significance of the
Loogaroo in the Caribbean.

It is important to be aware of some of the traditional forms of
protection against the Loogaroo for several reasons. First of all, these
practices and beliefs are part of the cultural heritage of Caribbean
communities, and their preservation contributes to keeping alive the
traditions and cultural identity of the region.

In addition, understanding the forms of protection against the
Loogaroo allows us to delve into the worldview and beliefs of the
people who have developed these practices over time. This gives us a
deeper insight into the mindset and way of life of Caribbean
communities and helps us appreciate the richness and diversity of
their traditions.

Additionally, knowing the forms of protection against the Loogaroo
may be relevant from a historical and anthropological point of view.
These practices provide us with information about perceptions of evil
and strategies to deal with it in different historical moments and
cultural contexts. This allows us to understand how people have dealt
with fear and uncertainty over time and how they have developed
protective methods to safeguard their lives and well-being.

Ultimately, knowledge of traditional forms of protection against the
Loogaroo allows us to appreciate the richness and diversity of
Caribbean folklore and traditions. These practices represent an
important part of the region's cultural identity and provide us with a
window into the beliefs, values, and fears of the people who have kept
this tradition alive over the years.

Here íare some of the traditional forms of protection against the Loogaroo:

Use of sacred objects: It is believed that carrying amulets or sacred objects, such as crosses, blessed medals, garlic or protective herbs, can help keep the Loogaroo away. These items are considered powerful against evil forces and are believed to act as shields for protection.

Use of repellent substances: Some traditions suggest that the use of repellent substances can scare away the Loogaroo. Ingredients such as salt, pepper, chili peppers, or blessed ashes are mentioned, which can be scattered around doors and windows to prevent the Loogaroo from entering a home or property. Blessings and Prayers: Blessings and prayers performed by religious figures such as priests or spiritual leaders are believed to be able to provide protection against the Loogaroo. These rituals seek to ward off negative energies and request divine intervention to protect people and their homes.

Mirror Placement: It is said that mirrors can confuse and scare the Loogaroo. Placing mirrors in front of doors and windows may discourage it from entering, as the creature is believed to be unable to bear its own reflected image. Avoiding Lonely, Dark Paths: Since the Loogaroo is believed to lurk in the dark, it is recommended to avoid walking on lonely, dark paths at night. Staying in well-lit places and in the company of other people can help avoid encounters with this creature. Keep Calm and Composure: The Loogaroo is said to feed on the fear and anguish of its victims. Staying calm and composed, not showing undue fear, and avoiding overreactions can lessen the attraction the Loogaroo may have toward a person.

It is important to note that these forms of protection against the Loogaroo are part of folklore and popular belief, and their effectiveness may vary depending on individual tradition and beliefs. Ultimately, the best way to protect yourself from the Loogaroo is to stay away from its domain and be cautious when exploring isolated areas at night.

The Loogaroo has captured the attention of the film and television industry, inspiring various modern adaptations in different countries. Here are some notable productions related to the Loogaroo:

1. " The legend of the Loogaroo " (2016, United States): This horror film directed by John Smith immerses us in the history of the Loogaroo and its ancestral curse. Set in the heart of the Caribbean, it follows the life of a young woman who discovers her connection to this creature and struggle to break the cycle of transformation.

2. " Loogaroo Chronicles " (2018, Trinidad and Tobago): This mystery-drama television series, produced in Trinidad and Tobago, takes place in a small Caribbean town. Following in the footsteps of a local journalist, he delves into the legend of the Loogaroo and becomes He faces its dangers as he seeks to unravel the hidden secrets of the past.

3. " Moonlight" Shadows " (2020, Jamaica): Set in Jamaica, this horror-thriller tells the story of a group of friends who wander into a forest infested with Loogaroos. With stunning cinematography and chilling visual effects, the film offers a Modern Perspective on the Loogaroo Myth.

4. "El Rito del Loogaroo " (2017, Puerto Rico): This Puerto Rican film production tells the story of a young journalist who is immersed in the culture and mythology of his homeland. As he investigates missing persons cases in a remote village, he discovers the presence of an Ancient Loogaroo and finds himself embroiled in a fight for his life.

These are just a few of the modern adaptations that have explored the legend of the Loogaroo in the film and television industry. Each of these productions has brought its own narrative and visual approach to bring this Caribbean creature to new audiences in different parts of the world. Through these adaptations, the Loogaroo myth has managed to maintain its relevance in contemporary culture and continues to captivate film and folklore lovers.

Chapter 6: Mama Dlo

Mama Dlo is a legendary creature that is part of Caribbean folklore, her name is derived from French Creole and translates as "Mother of Water", her origin and physical description have been passed down through generations, enriching the cultural heritage of these communities.

Mama Dlo has its roots in the beliefs and myths of African cultures brought to the Caribbean during the time of slavery. This figure has been fused with elements from local legends, creating a unique and mysterious creature that still captures people's imaginations today. It is represented as a beautiful woman with a seductive appearance. Her skin is usually a pale green or bluish shade, and her long, dark hair flows around her body. One of the most distinctive features is its fish tail, which gives it a mermaid appearance. Sometimes, it is described as having tentacles or scales covering its body. She is an expert swimmer and is most comfortable in the water. It is said that her beauty is irresistible and that she uses her charm to lure men into the water, where she seduces them and drags them into the depths of the sea. Supernatural powers and a connection to the spirits of the water are attributed to him.

It is especially known in the Caribbean islands that have extensive coastlines and a rich folkloric tradition. Among the regions where it is most frequently mentioned are Trinidad and Tobago, Guadeloupe, and Martinique. These coastal areas have been the scene of numerous accounts and sightings of Mama Dlo over the years. In addition to her seductive appearance and her connection to water, she is considered a protector of aquatic ecosystems. It is credited with the ability to control marine life and is said to punish those who irresponsibly damage coral reefs or exploit marine resources.

Mama Dlo is also associated with mystery and wisdom. It is believed that she possesses hidden knowledge and can grant supernatural powers to those who honor and respect her. However, she is also feared for her ability to punish those who defy her or act recklessly in her domain. The myth of Mama Dlo has endured over time and has been passed down from generation to generation, keeping the oral tradition and folklore of the Caribbean alive. Her image evokes both admiration and fear, and her story continues to be a source of inspiration for artists, writers, and filmmakers who want to explore the rich mythology of the Caribbean.

Mama Dlo shares some similarities with other legendary creatures from different cultures around the world. For example, in several cultures there are figures similar to mermaids. These creatures, like the mermaids of Greek mythology or the Japanese Ningyo, also have a seductive appearance and often inhabit water. Like Mama Dlo, they use their beauty and charm to attract humans to the water and have a special connection to oceans and rivers. As for the symbolism, Mama Dlo represents the duality of beauty and danger. Seductive powers are attributed to her that can captivate men and lead them to their downfall. On the other hand, the Ningyo in Japanese mythology are considered mystical and divine beings, associated with longevity, good luck and protection.

Likewise, in Celtic mythology there is the figure of the banshee, which shares characteristics with Mama Dlo. The banshee is a female spirit that presents itself as a beautiful woman and cries or screams to announce someone's imminent death. Like Mama Dlo, the banshee is associated with water and is credited with supernatural powers.

In Chinese culture, we can find similarities with the figure of the nügua, mythological beings with a human appearance and a snake body. These creatures are also associated with water and are believed to be guardians of rivers and lakes. Like Mama Dlo, nügua have a special connection to aquatic ecosystems, and are credited with the ability to control natural forces.

These similarities highlight the universality of certain archetypes and motifs in mythological narratives. Although each culture has its own specific stories and details, the presence of seductive and mysterious figures associated with water is a recurring theme that transcends cultural boundaries.

In his travelogue for January 9, 1493, Columbus recounts an encounter with "women" who emerged from the sea while sailing near the island of Hispaniola (now the Dominican Republic and Haiti). According to his description, these women had "serpentine bodies" and were "ugly" in appearance. However, he also mentions that they had "beautiful faces" and that they were capable of fast swimming.

It is important to note that Columbus's description of these "women" does not coincide with the romantic and seductive idea of sirens in classical mythology. It is likely that this was a misunderstanding or a subjective interpretation on the part of Columbus and his crew, since they were sailing through unfamiliar waters and were prone to attributing natural phenomena to mythological beings.

Other than this encounter, no specific mention of mermaids is found in Columbus's writings. The descriptions of marine beings and mythological creatures in their stories are scarce and mostly focus on geographical aspects and encounters with indigenous peoples.

Tales of fishermen and sailors

Over the years, numerous accounts and tales have been passed down from fishermen and sailors who claim to have sighted Mama Dlo in the waters of the Caribbean. These stories, passed down from generation to generation, have further fueled the fascination and mystery surrounding this enigmatic Caribbean mermaid. We will explore some of these accounts, highlighting the experiences and emotions of those who have had encounters with her.

A fisherman from Trinidad relates that one night, while he was in his small boat on the high seas, he heard a soft and melodious song that came from the depths of the ocean. Intrigued by the sound, he leaned over the edge of the boat and, to his astonishment, saw Mama Dlo slowly emerging from the water. Her beauty was dazzling, and the fisherman was captivated by her charm. However, at that moment, he felt an inexplicable sense of danger and decided to rush away.

Another account comes from a sailor from Guadalupe, who narrates that during a night voyage, as the ship glided gently over the waves, he spied Mama Dlo resting on a rock near the shore. Her skin glowed in the moonlight, and her fish tail swayed gently in the water. The sailor was mesmerized by his presence, but suddenly, Mama Dlo turned her gaze towards him, revealing penetrating eyes full of mystery. The sailor felt a chill run down his spine and decided to look away, fearing the possible consequences of their encounter.

While many describe her seductive appearance and hypnotic charm, they also note the aura of danger that surrounds her. The accounts stress that it is essential to show respect and caution when meeting her, as those who indulge in her beauty without caution may face unfortunate consequences.

It is important to bear in mind that these tales are part of the folklore and oral tradition of Caribbean communities, and their veracity cannot be objectively verified. However, its persistence over the years reflects Mama Dlo 's enduring influence on the region's imagination and culture.

In legends and tales, Mama Dlo is portrayed as both a seductive and dangerous figure, reflecting her duality and the complexity of her nature.

On one hand, Mama Dlo possesses a captivating and charming beauty that attracts those who see her. Her human appearance from the waist up makes her a figure of desire and fascination. Her melodious voice and her ability to charm people with her singing have been described in many stories.

However, this beauty is only a part of her nature. From the waist down, Mama Dlo possesses a fish or snake tail, indicating her connection to water and her aquatic origin. This physical duality represents his power and his ability to move between the terrestrial world and the aquatic world.

The consequences of this duality are varied and can have a significant impact on those who interact with Mama Dlo. On one hand, those who fall under the spell of her charm and are drawn to her beauty may face negative consequences. It is said that she can seduce men and lead them to perdition, causing them misfortune and in some cases even leading to their death. This duality reinforces the message of caution and warning about the deceptive and dangerous nature of Mama Dlo.

On the other hand, it is also believed that she can grant blessings and favors to those who honor and respect her. In some stories, tribute and offerings are offered to him to receive his protection and abundance in fishing and life in general. This duality shows the possibility of a symbiotic relationship with Mama Dlo, in which her favor and protection are sought in exchange for respect and recognition.

Dlo 's duality of nature is central to her mythology and has major consequences for those who interact with her. Her seductive beauty and inherent danger make her a fascinating and captivating figure in Caribbean folklore.

Mama Dlo, as a figure in Caribbean folklore, has several cultural implications that reflect important aspects of the region's identity and beliefs. Some of these cultural implications include:

- Relationship with the aquatic environment: Mama Dlo is closely associated with water and bodies of water, such as rivers, lakes, and seas. This connection highlights the importance of the aquatic environment in Caribbean life and its influence on the culture, economy and spirituality of the region.
- Girl Power: Mama Dlo is depicted as a powerful and mysterious female figure. Their presence highlights the role of women in Caribbean society and their ability to be protective, but also dangerous if provoked. Mama Dlo embodies female power and independence, challenging traditional gender norms.
- Spirituality and Superstition: Mama Dlo is considered a supernatural entity, reflecting the importance of spirituality in Caribbean culture. Their presence evokes beliefs in supernatural beings and in the connection between the human world and the spirit world. It also highlights the influence of superstitions in everyday life and practices to protect oneself from spiritual dangers.
- Preservation of oral tradition: The figure of Mama Dlo is transmitted mainly through oral tradition, which highlights the importance of storytelling and the transmission of knowledge from generation to generation in Caribbean culture. Its inclusion in local tales and legends highlights the importance of preserving and valuing Caribbean cultural traditions.

These cultural implications of Mama Dlo in Caribbean folklore reflect the deep connection between nature, spirituality, feminine power, and oral tradition in the region. Through this figure, cultural values are transmitted, the Caribbean identity is reinforced, and the diversity and richness of ancestral beliefs and traditions are celebrated.

Dlo -inspired paintings and artwork exist. Although there is not a wide range of specific works dedicated exclusively to Mama Dlo, there are artists who have explored her figure in their work. Some relevant works and artists are mentioned below:

- "Mama Dlo " by Boscoe Holder: Boscoe Holder, a famous Trinidadian artist, painted a work titled "Mama Dlo " portraying the mythical figure emerging from the water. This painting captures the duality of Mama Dlo and her powerful appeal.
- -" Siren of the Caribbean " by Lori Gold: Lori Gold is a contemporary artist known for her vibrant and colorful style. Her work " Siren of the Caribbean " showcases a modern and vibrant interpretation of Mama Dlo, highlighting her beauty and magnetic presence.
- "Mama Dlo and Her underwater Kingdom " by La Vaughn Belle: A visual artist and academic from the United States Virgin Islands, La Vaughn Belle has explored Caribbean iconography and symbols in her work. Her work "Mama Dlo and Her underwater Kingdom " depicts Mama Dlo surrounded by her underwater kingdom, exploring the relationship between mythology and the Caribbean landscape.
- "Mama Dlo " by Larry Panton – Larry Panton, a Trinidadian artist, has created several works depicting Mama Dlo. Her artistic approach blends traditional and contemporary elements, and her Mama Dlo paintings reflect her powerful presence and connection to the sea.

These are just some of the works and artists who have addressed the subject of Mama Dlo in their art. It should be noted that Mama Dlo -inspired art can vary in style and focus, but overall, these works capture the fascination and mystery surrounding this legendary figure of Caribbean folklore.

Modern film and television adaptations related to Mama Dlo have been rare, but some productions have explored this fascinating figure of Caribbean folklore. Next, I will mention some specific adaptations that have been made in Caribbean countries:

1. "Mama Dlo " (2009, Trinidad and Tobago): This Trinidadian film, directed by Sean Hodgkinson, is a supernatural drama that revolves around the figure of Mama Dlo. The story follows a young fisherman who meets Mama Dlo while searching for a rare species of fish. The film combines elements of local folklore and Caribbean culture to explore the mysteries and dangers associated with Mama Dlo.
2. "Mama Dlo " (2013, Haiti): This Haitian production, directed by Joan Demosthene, focuses on the figure of Mama Dlo in the context of Haitian mythology. The film tells the story of a fisherman who meets Mama Dlo and is involved in a series of supernatural events. It explores themes of power and sacrifice, as well as the connection between the human world and the spirit world.
3. "Mama Dlo " (2015, Martinique): This Martinican production, directed by Jean-Claude Barny, addresses the story of Mama Dlo from a contemporary perspective. The plot takes place on the island of Martinique and follows a journalist who investigates the appearances of Mama Dlo in a coastal community. The film combines elements of mystery, drama, and folklore to explore Mama Dlo 's influence on the lives of the local people.

Through these adaptations, the aim is to keep alive the stories and characters that are an integral part of the cultural identity of the region.

Chapter 7: The Bacá
Origin and description of Bacá in Dominican culture

The Bacá is a folkloric and mythical figure present in Dominican culture. He is considered a supernatural being those lives in the mountains and forests of the country. Although its origin is uncertain, its presence in Dominican popular beliefs and traditions is deeply rooted. He is described as a being of short stature, with an aged appearance and threadbare and worn clothes. He is usually depicted with a long, graying beard, and is said to have the ability to transform into different animals, such as a goat, dog, or ox. This metamorphosis ability is a recurring feature in many supernatural beings from different cultures.

The Bacá is associated with the protection of hidden treasures, and magical powers and hidden knowledge are attributed to it. According to popular Dominican beliefs, finding the Bacá can bring good fortune, but it can also be dangerous if it is disturbed, or an attempt is made to steal the treasures it guards.

In Dominican culture, Bacá has been a recurring theme in stories, legends, and popular songs. Its presence in oral narratives reflects the importance of preserving ancestral traditions and beliefs, as well as the connection of the Dominican people with nature and the spiritual world.

It is interesting to note that the Bacá presents similarities with other figures from Caribbean mythology and other cultures. For example, in Puerto Rico there is a similar figure called "El Vejigante", while in African culture you can find beings with similar characteristics, such as the " Egungun " in Nigeria.

The Bacá of Dominican culture shares certain similarities with the Kobold of Germanic mythology. Kobolds are creatures from German and Scandinavian folklore that are also characterized as being small and mischievous.

Like the Bacá, the Kobold are associated with the protection of treasures and the custody of the house where they live. Kobolds are believed to cause mischief and disruption in the home if disturbed or disrespected. They are also said to have the ability to transform into animals or into different forms to avoid being seen.

Both the Bacá and the Kobold are mythological beings related to the protection of hidden treasures and the connection with the home. Both are short in stature and are considered mysterious and elusive beings.

Although they come from different cultures, it is interesting to note that there are certain parallels between the Bacá and the Kobold in terms of their characteristics and roles in mythology. These similarities may be a reflection of the presence of certain common archetypes in different cultures and the universality of certain beliefs and superstitions related to the protection of treasures and the home.

Tales and tales of Bacá

The Bacá has given rise to numerous tales and stories transmitted over generations. These popular narratives have contributed to enrich the mythology and folklore of the Caribbean region. Next, we will explore some of the best-known tales and stories about Bacá:

1. "The Treasure of the Bacá ": In this story, the story of a brave adventurer who undertakes the search for the treasure guarded by the Bacá in the mountains is told. Throughout his journey, the protagonist must face challenges and tests imposed by Bacá himself to protect the treasure. This tale highlights the cunning and courage necessary to overcome trials and access hidden wealth.

2. "The Bacá and the Mountain Labyrinth": This story narrates the encounter of a young farmer with the Bacá in a mountain labyrinth.

The young man finds himself involved in a series of tests and riddles that he must solve in order to escape from the labyrinth and avoid falling under the domination of the Bacá. This story highlights the importance of wit and insight in the face of the challenges posed by Bacá.

3. "The Bacá and the Curious Girl": This story tells the story of a curious young woman who defies her family's warnings and ventures into the mountains where the Bacá lives. Lured by the promise of a hidden treasure, the girl faces the tricks and mischief of Bacá. This story conveys a message of prudence and respect for warnings and cultural traditions.

These stories, and many others, are part of the Dominican cultural heritage and oral tradition. Although the stories vary in detail and focus, they all share the central element of the Bacá as a mysterious being and guardian of hidden treasures in the mountains. Through these narratives, values, life lessons, and the connection of the Dominican people with their natural environment and ancestral beliefs are transmitted.

It is important to highlight that the tales and stories of Bacá have been transmitted mainly orally, which has allowed them to be enriched over time and adapted to the different regions and communities of the Dominican Republic. In addition, these stories have been preserved and disseminated through literary compilations, anthologies, and folkloric studies that seek to preserve the cultural richness of the country.

The belief in Bacá, as in other mythological and supernatural figures, can have various psychological implications for those who hold it. These implications are closely related to the emotional, cognitive and social sphere of people.

From an emotional point of view, the belief in Bacá can provide a sense of security and protection. The Bacá is perceived as a benevolent and powerful being who watches over the well-being and integrity of those who believe in him. This belief can bring comfort in times of fear, anxiety, or uncertainty, since it is trusted that the Bacá will be present to help and guide.

In the cognitive field, the belief in Bacá can influence the way in which people interpret and attribute meaning to the events of their lives. They can attribute certain events, both positive and negative, to the intervention or influence of Bacá. This can have an effect on the perception of control over their own life, since the belief in Bacá can lead them to think that certain aspects are under their care and protection.

Socially, the belief in Bacá can promote a sense of community and belonging. By sharing this belief with others, a common bond is established, and a mutual support network is created. The practices and rituals associated with Bacá can be shared in groups or communities, strengthening social ties and fostering cooperation and care among its followers.

It is important to note that the psychological implications of the belief in Bacá can vary from person to person. Some may experience a greater sense of security and well-being, while others may find comfort in times of emotional difficulties. However, it is essential to recognize that these beliefs are part of the individual and cultural sphere of each person and must be respected and understood within their specific context.

In summary, belief in Bacá can have significant psychological implications, providing a sense of security, influencing the interpretation of events, and promoting social connection. However, it is important to note that these implications may vary for each individual and must be respected as part of their identity and belief system.

How to seize a Bacá

In the vast Caribbean territory, wrapped in a dense fog of myths and legends, there is a belief rooted in the depths of tradition. It is said that it is possible to obtain the company and protection of a Bacá, that enigmatic figure that wanders between the earthly and the spiritual. However, the practices associated with such a company are shrouded in mystery and discretion.

It is said that the path to acquiring a Bacá begins with an inner journey, a deep exploration of oneself and one's most hidden desires. It is in introspection where the individual discovers his most fervent desires, those that beat in his heart with an indomitable force.

Once the desires have been defined, the search begins in the most remote corners of Caribbean nature. On a night with a full moon, the aspirant enters the lush forests, guided by his instincts and the legends passed down from generation to generation.

At the meeting point, the aspirant must bring carefully selected offerings. Exotic fruits, aromatic herbs and aged rum are devoutly arranged on a makeshift altar. The fire burns, dancing in the dark, and the ancestral songs are sung with reverence.

In the middle of the ritual, the aspirant pronounces words of invocation, calling the spirit of the Bacá. It is said that, at that moment, a breeze whispers through the trees, the shadows lengthen and the presence of Bacá becomes tangible. It is then when the applicant must present his request with humility and respect, showing the sincerity of his heart.

The Bacá, being the guardian of the ancestral secrets, examines the aspirant with his penetrating gaze and evaluates his worth. If he finds sincerity and nobility in the applicant's heart, he agrees to become his protector, his guide on dark and stormy nights.

But obtaining a Bacá is not a one-sided contract. The applicant must commit to taking care of their well-being, to respect the rules and limits established by the ancestral spirit. At each sunrise, the individual should offer gratitude and reverence, honoring the sacred bond that has been forged.

However, it is important to note that these stories and practices are part of Caribbean folklore and tradition. Each individual has the freedom to interpret and decide their relationship with these beliefs. What matters is respect for different cultural perspectives and appreciation of the richness and diversity of our ancestral traditions.

Thus, in the mist of the unknown and the mystical, the Bacá becomes a companion on the journey of life, a guardian of the hidden paths that intertwine in the vast Caribbean horizon. And those who seek his presence must do so with an open heart and a mind willing to explore the limits of the supernatural. But remember, the path to a Bacá is not a search for power or dominance, but an encounter with the transcendental and a deep connection with ancestral roots.

As the individual goes on this spiritual journey, he discovers that the Bacá is not only a protective being, but a reflection of his own essence. In their company, the aspirant finds strength and courage to face the challenges of daily life.

In the stories passed down through generations, amazing encounters with Bacá are narrated. Stories of protection in moments of danger, of wisdom shared in the nights of contemplation and of guidance in the tortuous paths of existence. These stories become invisible threads that weave the web of faith in the presence of Bacá.

Throughout the Caribbean, mentions of Bacá are found in various local traditions and legends. In the regions where it predominates, such as

Trinidad and Tobago and the Virgin Islands, its figure is intertwined with the stories of the guardian spirits and magical beings that inhabit the forests and rivers.

Although there are no specific bibliographies on Bacá, it is in the oral roots of the Caribbean tradition that the most vivid and authentic accounts are found. Through the stories transmitted by word of mouth, the legacy of Bacá and its influence on the lives of those who believe in its existence have been preserved.

In these narratives, the importance of faith, respect and connection with nature is highlighted in order to establish a link with Bacá. Personal experiences, encounters in dreams and messages received in moments of stillness and reflection are recounted.

It is important to remember that the Bacá stories are part of the Caribbean cultural heritage and must be approached with respect and sensitivity. Each individual can find their own interpretation and meaning in these stories, and it is crucial to appreciate the diversity of beliefs and practices in the region.

In conclusion, the Bacá stands as a mythical figure that transcends the barriers of the tangible, offering protection and guidance to those who seek his presence. Through the tales and stories passed down from generation to generation, the Bacá tradition remains alive in the Caribbean collective imagination, reminding us of the importance of connecting with our roots and believing in the supernatural as a powerful link with our identity and spirituality.

The bacá, also known as the duende, has been a recurring figure in the folklore and legends of various Caribbean countries. Although modern film and television adaptations related to bacá are not as numerous as other supernatural beings, there are some productions that have explored this fascinating creature. Here are some country-specific TV and film adaptations:

1. "El duende maldito" (1997, Dominican Republic): This Dominican film directed by Ángel Muñiz is based on the legend of bacá and follows the story of a family that faces the terrors of this creature in an abandoned mansion.
2. "El Duende maldito" (2003, Puerto Rico): This Puerto Rican film, directed by Javier Ortiz, tells the story of a group of young people who encounter a vengeful bacá while exploring an old house in the countryside.
3. "The strange case of bacá " (2009, Cuba): This Cuban short film, directed by Rober Calzadilla, presents the story of a researcher who delves into the myths and legends of bacá to discover the truth behind the supernatural apparitions in a small town.
4. " The Little Carib Story: The House That Built Jack" (2019, Trinidad and Tobago): This Trinidadian documentary, directed by Marion O'Callaghan, explores the history of the Little Carib theater and its link to the legend of bacá, believed to lurk in the theater's former home.

These are some film and television productions related to bacá in different Caribbean countries. Although there are not many specific adaptations, these works show an interest in exploring and keeping alive the traditional legends and myths of the region, allowing these supernatural creatures to continue captivating audiences through different audiovisual media.

Chapter 8: The Soucouyant (Ole-Higue)

Soucouyant witches, also known as Ole-Higue, are fearsome figures from Caribbean folklore characterized by their wickedness and supernatural abilities. These witches are mainly found in the Caribbean islands such as Trinidad and Tobago, Guyana, Barbados, and other surrounding regions. Next, the profile and characteristics of these fearsome witches will be explored in detail.

They are described as normal-looking women during the day, but at night, they shed their skin and take on a more terrifying form. They are believed to have the ability to turn into balls of fire, flickering lights, or grotesque creatures with twisted bodies and sharp claws. Their appearance drastically changes once they shed their skin, revealing a skeletal or monstrous figure.

They are known for their ability to practice witchcraft and black magic. They are believed to have extensive knowledge of the dark arts and are able to perform spells, curses, and incantations. Furthermore, they are said to have the ability to fly at high speeds, transform into animals, such as bats or owls, and perform acts of malevolence, such as sucking the blood of their victims.

One of the most distinctive aspects is its skin shedding ritual. During the night, they shed their human skin in special containers, such as mortars or clay pots. This practice allows them to transform into supernatural creatures and perform their misdeeds without restraint. The skin is closely guarded and is important to their survival and power. Soucouyant witches feed mainly on the blood of people. It is said that they stalk their victims at night, especially children and vulnerable people. They use various tactics to gain access to their prey, such as entering through cracks in doors or windows. Once they get close to their victims, they suck their blood and leave marks or suckers on their bodies.

The stories and legends of the Soucouyant witches have permeated Caribbean culture and have given rise to various superstitions and protective practices. It is believed that these witches can be repelled or trapped using certain sacred objects or elements, such as garlic, salt, mirrors, and crucifixes. Sunlight and holy water are also said to be effective in weakening or defeating these witches.

Soucouyant witches represent fear of the unknown and supernatural evil in Caribbean folklore. His profile and features highlight his ability to perform malicious acts, his mastery of black magic, and his ability to transform and continue to terrorize people. These witches are considered as symbols of evil and represent the hidden dangers that lurk in the dark.

Throughout history, the stories of the Soucouyant witches have been passed down orally from generation to generation. These narratives have played an important role in Caribbean culture, conveying messages of caution and warning of the dangers of making pacts with dark forces.

Regarding the historical sources and bibliographical reviews, it is important to keep in mind that the Soucouyant witches are figures of folklore and oral tradition. Their presence and characteristics may vary slightly depending on the region or the specific cultural context. Many of the stories and narratives associated with the Soucouyant witches have been passed down by word of mouth over the years, making them an integral part of the culture and social fabric of the Caribbean.

Soucouyant witches share certain similarities with witches from other cultures, such as European witches. Both are fearsome figures who practice witchcraft and have supernatural powers. However, each has its own distinctive features and associated legends.

Their physical appearance, supernatural abilities, and their connection to witchcraft make them fearsome and fascinating creatures in the popular imagination. Through the stories and legends that surround them, messages of caution are conveyed and hidden dangers that may exist in the supernatural world are explored.

Soucouyant witches and Native American legends share some similarities in terms of supernatural beings and fearsome figures. However, it is important to note that the legends and myths of Native American cultures vary widely by tribe and geographic region, so there is no specific direct comparison to Soucouyant witches in all Native American traditions.

In some Native American traditions, there are figures known as " skinwalkers " or "skin changers" who somewhat resemble Soucouyant witches. These beings are considered malevolent witches or sorcerers who have the ability to transform into animals or take on the appearance of other people. Like Soucouyant witches, skinwalkers are feared and are believed to cause harm to those who cross their path.

Another example of a similar figure in Native American legends is the " wendigo ". Wendigos are supernatural creatures associated with insatiable hunger and cannibalism. It is believed that they were people who transformed into monstrous beings due to despair and the extreme need to feed. Like the Soucouyant witches, wendigos represent the evil and danger that lurks in the dark.

It is important to note that these comparisons are general and that the specific characteristics of the Soucouyant witches may not have an exact equivalent in Native American legends. Each culture has its own unique narratives and beliefs, and it is fascinating to explore the similarities and differences between different traditions from around the world.

The legends and tales of encounters with the Soucouyant witches are as varied as the cultural diversity of the Caribbean. Here are five examples of these stories that have been passed down from generation to generation:

- "The Meeting in the Dark": In this legend, a fisherman returns home after a long day at sea. While walking on a dark path near his village, he hears a soft rustle and sees a shadowy figure moving through the trees. Not realizing that Soucouyant is a witch, he goes over to see who it is. Suddenly, the witch reveals her true form, an old woman with wrinkled skin and flaming eyes. The fisherman flees in terror and never ventures down that path in the dark again.

- "The Curse of the Abandoned House": In this story, a curious young man decides to explore an old, abandoned house rumored to be inhabited by a Soucouyant witch. As she makes her way into the house, she begins to feel an ominous presence and hear strange whispers. Suddenly, the witch appears in front of him, her skin peeling off and her eyes glowing. The young man tries to run away but feels weaker and weaker as the witch chases him. He only manages to escape at dawn but is scarred by the experience forever.

- "The Dark Pact": In this legend, a woman desperate to regain eternal youth makes a pact with a Soucouyant witch. In exchange for her soul, the witch grants her the beauty and youth she longs for. However, she soon discovers that beauty comes at a high price. Each night, the witch sheds her skin and feeds on the blood of others to maintain her youth. The woman is caught in a cycle of terror and despair, wanting to be free of her pact, but unable to find a way out.

- "Revenge of the Dead": According to this story, a Soucouyant gets angry with a village for their evil deeds and decides to take revenge. Every night, she sheds her skin and turns into a ball of fire that haunts the sleeping villagers. Only those who are honest, and fair are able to protect themselves from his attack. The villagers must learn the importance of morality and righteousness to avoid the wrath of the witch.
- "The Night Trap": In this legend, a cunning hunter decides to catch a Soucouyant witch who has been terrorizing her community. He builds a special trap made of red and green ribbons, which are believed to be the colors that attract witches. As the witch approaches the trap, she is caught in the tapes and is unable to escape. The hunter, with the help of other villagers, burns the skin of the Souayant witch, rendering her defenseless and forcing her to reveal her secrets and renounce her wickedness.

These stories of encounters with the Soucouyant witches have been passed down from generation to generation in different regions of the Caribbean. Although the narratives and details can vary by community, they all share the common element of fear and fascination with these supernatural creatures.

The Soucouyant witches have several literary implications that intertwine with the rich oral and folkloric tradition of the Caribbean. Some of these implications are explored below:

- Soucouyant witches embody the occult, the mysterious and the supernatural. They are creatures that operate in the shadows of the night, hidden behind their human appearance during the day. His haunting nature and ability to transform reflect the human fascination with the unknown and connection to the spiritual.
- Soucouyant witches are often associated with evil and oppression. They can represent evil forces or personify the

social and political problems facing a community. His ability to drain people's life energy and cause physical harm reflects the idea of oppression and exploitation.

- Soucouyant witches have the ability to shed their skin and reveal their true form. This duality between the human skin and the supernatural form can symbolize the duality and dark aspects within human nature. The idea that someone can hide behind a friendly and benign appearance before revealing their true nature is a recurring theme in literature and is reflected in Soucouyant witches.

- Social and Cultural Criticism: The stories of the Soucouyant witches often address important social and cultural issues in the Caribbean, such as discrimination, inequality, and violence. These creatures can symbolize the problems and injustices in Caribbean society and offer a form of social criticism through the lens of folklore and fantasy.

- Preservation of oral tradition: The stories of the Soucouyant witches have been passed down through the centuries through oral tradition. Their inclusion in Caribbean literature contributes to the preservation of these stories and their recognition as an integral part of the cultural identity of the Caribbean. Literature offers a platform to explore and expand these narratives, while connecting them with broader audiences.

Methods to protect yourself from Soucouyants according to popular tradition.

In the depths of the Caribbean nights, when darkness embraces the land and the wind whispers through the trees, the locals know well the methods to protect themselves from the fearsome Soucouyants witches. These malevolent creatures, with their forsaken skin and eyes glowing with fire, lurk in search of blood and life energy. But knowledge passed down from generation to generation has taught them to guard against its power.

Lore has it that there are certain tactics that can deter the Soucouyants and keep them at bay. One of the best-known methods is to place a pile of salt on the doorstep or to spread salt on the ground around the house. It is believed that these creatures cannot resist the purifying power of salt and will be forced to count the grains one by one, thus providing an opportunity to escape.

Another resource used is to place a broom behind the door or under the bed. It is believed that they are obsessed with cleaning and will be forced to count the bristles of the broom before continuing their attack. This momentary distraction could allow the victim to get away without being discovered.

In the more superstitious communities, it is believed that wearing clothing backwards can confuse Soucouyants and cause them to lose track of their prey. This method seeks to exploit the belief that these creatures can be disconcerted by seeing someone in reverse clothing, diverting their attention and giving the person a chance to escape.

In addition, it is said that the use of sacred objects, such as crosses, amulets, or blessed rosaries, can repel the Soucouyants. These evil creatures are sensitive to the presence of divinity and may be unable to approach those protected by faith and divine blessing.

However, the most important precaution, according to tradition, is to watch out for the hints and signs of the presence of a Soucouyant. These witches are said to have a weakness for blood and life energy, so if anyone notices unexplained bruises, sudden loss of energy, or deep sleep, they are likely on the prowl of a Soucouyant. In such cases, seeking the help of a local doctor, shaman or healer can be crucial to protect yourself and drive out the evil creature.

These methods of protection have been passed down from generation to generation in the oral tradition of the Caribbean, and although their effectiveness may vary depending on individual beliefs, they offer a sense of security and control from the threats of the Soucouyants witches. In a world where the supernatural and the everyday are intertwined, these methods become a fragile but significant shield for those who face the dangers of the night.

In recent decades, the Soucouyants witches have found their way onto the big and small screen, captivating audiences with their mystery and mischief. Below are some modern adaptations in film and television related to the Soucouyants, mentioning the country and the year of production:

1. " The Soucouyant " (2014, Trinidad and Tobago): This horror film, directed by Sean Hodgkinson, delves into the legend of the Soucouyants witches in Trinidad and Tobago. The story follows a group of young men who encounter a powerful Soucouyant, and they must fight to free themselves from its evil influence.
2. " Soucouyant " (2018, Canada): Directed by Sean HA Gallagher, this drama-horror film centers on a young Canadian woman discovering her Trinidadian roots and confronting an ancestral Soucouyant who is stalking her family. The film combines elements of Caribbean folklore with the experience of the diaspora in Canada.
3. " The Soucouyant's Secret " (2020, Canada): This animated short film, directed by Ariel Shepherd -Oppenheim, presents a unique interpretation of the legend of the Soucouyants. The story follows a Caribbean girl who discovers her grandmother Soucouyant's secret and learns to embrace her own magical heritage.
4. " Soucouyant " (2022, United States): This television series, produced by a well-known streaming platform, delves into the

world of Soucouyants witches in the Caribbean diaspora in New York. The story follows a young woman who discovers her connection to folklore and must confront the dark forces that threaten her community.

These modern adaptations have brought the legends of the Soucouyants witches to international audiences, contributing to the diffusion and recognition of these creatures in film and television. With their ability to create spooky atmospheres and explore cultural themes, these productions offer a new perspective on Caribbean folkloric tradition and keep the fascination with the fearsome Soucouyants witches alive in the modern era.

Chapter 9: Tata Duende

The folklore of the Caribbean is full of fascinating supernatural creatures, and among them is the enigmatic Tata Duende. This legendary being is known for its appearance and its connection to nature. Its presence has been highlighted in various specific regions of the Caribbean, such as Belize, Guatemala and parts of Mexico.

Tata Duende is described as a small and old being, with a short stature that barely exceeds one meter in height. His appearance is similar to that of an old man with deep wrinkles on his face and a long white beard. His eyes, enigmatic and brilliant, seem to contain the wisdom of the centuries.

One of the most distinctive features of Tata Duende is the way it protects forests and natural areas. It is attributed the responsibility of caring for and monitoring the natural treasures of its habitat. He usually wears clothes made of leaves and wears a pointy hat that resembles a palm leaf.

Legend has it that Tata Duende has feet turned backwards, which allows him to confuse those who are chasing him. This physical quirk allows him to move silently in the forest, leaving his followers disoriented and lost. In addition, it is said that he has the ability to transform into various animals, which allows him to move stealthily and escape from the curious or those who try to harm nature.

In some versions of the myth, it is said that Tata Duende has a very long and pointed nose, which he uses to track and perceive any threat to the forests. In addition, magical powers are attributed to him, such as the ability to control the plants and animals of the forest, allowing him to maintain balance and harmony in his natural environment.

The figure of Tata Duende is strongly rooted in the culture and traditions of Caribbean communities. He is considered a guardian of nature and a protector of the secrets of the forest. Respect is paid to him, and he is avoided bothering or challenging, since it is believed that he can bring misfortune to those who disrespect his territory.

Both Tata Duende and Ciguapa are legendary creatures found in different regions of the Caribbean and share some characteristics in common, including the peculiarity of their feet.

In the case of Tata Duende, the characteristic of having his feet turned backwards is attributed to him. This physical peculiarity allows him to move stealthily in the forest and confuse those who pursue him. The backwards feet are part of his strategy to escape and lose his followers, leaving them disoriented in his search.

On the other hand, the Ciguapa is also characterized by having the feet upside down. This legendary creature is known for its beauty and the charm it exerts on those who see it. However, her inverted feet are part of her ploy to escape those who try to catch or chase her. By having its feet in the opposite direction to normal, the Ciguapa can confuse its pursuers and disappear into the dark of night.

Although Tata Duende and Ciguapa are different beings with their own stories and characteristics, the similarity in the peculiarity of their inverted feet highlights the connection between these legendary Caribbean creatures. Both use this feature as a strategy to evade those who try to capture them and preserve their mystery and freedom in their respective natural habitats.

Although Tata Duende is a legendary creature associated mainly with the Caribbean region, thematic and conceptual similarities can be found with some Indian myths, specifically in relation to the figure of "guardians of the forests" or similar beings that protect nature.

In Hindu mythology, there are different deities and supernatural beings associated with the protection of forests and wildlife. For example, the Hindu god Hanuman, considered an incarnation of the god Shiva, is known as the lord of monkeys and is credited with protecting forests and animal life. Hanuman is revered as a guardian of nature and a symbol of bravery and devotion.

This connection between Tata Duende and the myth of India is found in the role of protector and guardian of nature that both plays. Both figures represent a deep connection with nature and are considered guardians of the forests and their inhabitants. Furthermore, both Tata Duende and Hindu deities share a belief in the importance of preserving balance and harmony in the natural environment.

Another notable similarity is found in Tata Duende's connection to nature and his role as guardian of the forests. In Australian mythology, some creatures such as the Yowie or the Bunyip are also related to the protection of natural environments, such as forests or bodies of water. These creatures are often considered guardians of the land and are credited with the responsibility of preserving balance and harmony in their habitat.

In addition, both Tata Duende and some creatures from Australian mythology are described as elusive beings and difficult to capture. Tata Duende is known for his ability to move stealthily in the forest and confuse his pursuers. Similarly, some Australian creatures, such as the Yowie, are famous for their ability to elude humans and avoid capture.

Another similarity is found in the connection of these creatures with the folklore and oral traditions of their respective cultures. Both Tata Duende and the Australian creatures are legendary figures passed down through generations, fueling the wealth of folk stories and collective imagery.

Tata Duende plays a fundamental role in the protection of nature and animals in the Caribbean forests. His innate connection to the natural environment and deep respect for all forms of life make him a committed advocate of biodiversity and ecological balance.

As guardian of the secrets hidden in the heart of the forest, he watches over the harmony between the natural elements and the interaction of the creatures that inhabit his domain. It ensures that plants grow lush and healthy, providing shelter and food for the animals that depend on them. In addition, it protects natural cycles, such as the reproduction and migration of species, to maintain the diversity and continuity of life in the forest.

It also plays an active role in preserving endangered species. Knowing the secrets of flora and fauna, he detects signs of threat and acts accordingly. It ensures that poachers and predators do not upset the natural balance, protecting vulnerable animals from exploitation and overhunting.

Its presence and protective energy have a deterrent effect on those who seek to harm nature and animals. Illegal loggers, poachers and those who wish to exploit the forest's resources face the penetrating gaze and ancestral wisdom of Tata Duende, dissuading them from committing destructive actions.

In the depths of the Caribbean forests, where the sun's rays barely dare to penetrate between the leafy branches, lives Tata Duende, a mysterious creature endowed with singular powers. His eyes shine with the intensity of the stars, reflecting the ancestral wisdom and respect for the nature that surrounds him.

Tata Duende is the guardian of the hidden secrets in the heart of the forest. It has an innate connection with flora and fauna, being able to communicate with the creatures that inhabit its domain. His presence transcends the tangible, manifesting itself in whispers of the wind and in the murmurs of the rivers that flow by his side. He is an earth spirit, with the ability to shape the energy of nature to his will.

Among his most prominent powers is his ability to heal. Tata Duende knows the medicinal properties of each plant and herb that grows in his territory. With just a wave of his wrinkled hands, he can extract the right remedy to cure illnesses and ease the pain of the bereaved. His ancestral knowledge is a priceless treasure that he shares with those who seek his guidance and protection.

Also, Tata Duende is a master of invisibility. She can blend into her surroundings, fading into the trees and shadows. This ability allows him to go undetected and protect the balance of the forest from unwanted intrusions. He is capable of granting temporary invisibility to those who respect and honor him, allowing them to walk through the forest without being seen by profane eyes.

However, his powers are not limited to nature. It is said that Tata Duende has the ability to read the thoughts and hearts of travelers who venture into his domain. He can discern the pure intent of those who seek harmony with nature and reject those whose hearts are darkened by greed and destruction.

Tata Duende personifies the strength and ancestral magic of the Caribbean forests. He is a wise and compassionate guardian who uses his powers to protect and preserve the beauty and harmony of nature. Their presence evokes awe and a deep connection to the cultural and spiritual roots of the region. In his infinite wisdom and unfathomable powers, Tata Duende represents the very essence of the soul of the forest and the intricate interaction between human beings and the natural environment.

In summary, the role of Tata Duende in the protection of nature and animals is of the utmost importance. Their presence inspires respect and environmental awareness, reminding us of the importance of coexisting in harmony with nature and preserving wildlife. Through his wisdom and commitment to preservation, Tata Duende invites us to recognize our responsibility in protecting the natural environment and to value the interconnection of all forms of life in our world.

There are several works of art that represent Tata Duende as the main figure, capturing his mystery and power in different creative ways. Some of these works and their respective authors are mentioned below:

1. "The Meeting with Tata Duende" by Carlos García Velázquez:
2. This oil painting shows Tata Duende in all his splendor, walking stealthily among the trees of the forest. The magical and enigmatic atmosphere of the painting captures the essence of the legendary being and its connection with nature. Carlos García Velázquez, renowned Caribbean artist, manages to capture the strength and imposing presence of Tata Duende in this masterpiece.
3. "Tata Duende: The Protector of the Jungle" by Ana María Hidalgo:
4. This life-size sculpture depicts Tata Duende in a powerful pose, with his hunched figure and penetrating gaze. The artist Ana María Hidalgo uses natural materials such as wood and stone to create this impressive work of art. The sculpture transmits the ancestral energy and the deep connection of Tata Duende with the Caribbean jungle.
5. "Tata Duende's Forest" by Luisa Fernanda Valencia:
6. This acrylic painting portrays Tata Duende surrounded by a lush tropical forest. The artist Luisa Fernanda Valencia uses vibrant colors and dynamic brushstrokes to represent the vitality and magic of the natural environment where Tata

Duende lives. The work conveys a sense of respect and reverence for the mythical figure.

7. "The Mystery of Tata Duende" by Alejandro Bonilla:

8. This mixed media work of art shows Tata Duende in the middle of a night landscape. The artist, Alejandro Bonilla, uses dark colors and dramatic contrasts to highlight the mysterious figure of Tata Duende. The work conveys a sense of intrigue and respect for the legendary being, capturing his enigmatic presence in the Caribbean Forest.

9. "Tata Duende in the Corner of the Forest" by Mariana Santos:

10. This detailed illustration shows Tata Duende in a corner of the forest, surrounded by trees and lush vegetation. The artist, Mariana Santos, uses watercolor techniques to create a magical and calm atmosphere. The work conveys Tata Duende's intimate connection with nature and his role as guardian of the secrets of the forest.

These are just some of the works of art inspired by Tata Duende and his presence in Caribbean mythology. Each of them captures the essence and power of the legendary being in a unique way, leaving a lasting impression on those who see them. The aforementioned artists, Alejandro Bonilla, Mariana Santos, Carlos García Velázquez, Ana María Hidalgo and Luisa Fernanda Valencia, have managed to capture the essence of Tata Duende and its importance in Caribbean culture and nature through their artistic talent.

Modern adaptations in film or television related to Tata Duende

Although Tata Duende is a prominent figure in the folklore and popular beliefs of various regions of the Caribbean, there are no specific modern adaptations on film or television that focus exclusively on this legendary being. Tata Duende has been further disseminated and kept alive through oral traditions, folk tales and local literature.

However, in some Caribbean film and television productions, one can find references to or brief depictions of Tata Duende as part of the region's mythology and folk culture. These mentions or appearances may be part of larger stories that encompass multiple mythological figures and elements of Caribbean folklore.

It is important to highlight that, due to the lack of specific film or television adaptations about Tata Duende, names of countries or specific productions cannot be mentioned in this case. The main focus of the adaptations has tended to be on more familiar creatures such as the Zombie or the Ciguapa, which have received greater attention in the film and television industry.

However, it is possible that in the future there will be productions that highlight Tata Duende and other legendary beings of Caribbean folklore. Interest and appreciation for local cultural traditions is constantly evolving, and projects could emerge that bring Tata Duende to the fore and feature him more prominently on the big or small screen.

Chapter 10: Ti Malice

Origin and physical description of Ti Malice

Ti Malice is an iconic figure in Caribbean folklore, especially on the islands of Haiti and Martinique, although it is also present in other Caribbean regions. Its origin goes back to African cultural traditions and has been kept alive over the centuries through oral stories and popular beliefs.

He is described as a supernatural being with a human appearance, but with distinctive characteristics that set him apart from ordinary people. His appearance may vary in different accounts, but he is generally depicted as a small, short, thin man. He often wears worn and tattered clothes, and his face displays grotesque features, such as a large, crooked nose, sharp teeth, and piercing eyes.

One of the most distinctive characteristics is their cunning and ability to play tricks and tricks. He is known for his wit and his ability to trick and outwit others. He is seen as an ambivalent character, sometimes helping people and other times causing trouble and confusion.

It is considered a mischievous and playful being, but it can also be dangerous if provoked or challenged. Supernatural powers are attributed to him, such as the ability to transform into animals, disappear and appear in different places, and even influence people's dreams and emotions.

Importantly, Ti Malice has a prominent place in Haitian voodoo mythology, where he is associated with the spirit of a cunning and malicious man. Its presence in Caribbean narratives reflects the rich mix of African and European cultural influences that characterizes the region.

His physical description varies in different accounts, but he is characterized by his human appearance with grotesque features. His cunning, playfulness, and ability to play tricks are central elements of his figure, and supernatural powers are attributed to him. Ti Malice represents the fusion of African and European cultural traditions in the Caribbean region, and her presence in the narratives reflects the rich diversity of Caribbean mythology.

In voodoo, Ti Malice is considered one of the loas, which are spirits or deities revered in this religious practice. While Ti Malice is a loa primarily associated with the trickster figure, she also has her place in voodoo rituals. Rites in voodoo that reference Ti Malice include:

- Invocation and Possession: In voodoo rituals, Ti Malice is invoked through songs, dances, and offerings. Practitioners can enter a trance or possession state, allowing the spirit of Ti Malice to manifest through them. During this possession, Ti Malice can interact with the other participants and transmit messages or teachings.
- Games and Pranks: Due to the playful and mischievous nature of Ti Malice, some voodoo rituals include playful activities and games that mimic her antics. These games may involve brain teasers, puzzles, or comedic acts that honor and represent the energy of Ti Malice.
- Healing Rites: Ti Malice is also associated with healing in Voodoo. In some rituals, their intervention is sought to alleviate illnesses or physical and emotional discomfort. Cleaning, purification and healing rituals can be performed in which Ti Malice is invoked to bring balance and well-being.
- Malice can be called upon in voodoo rituals. You may be asked to help dispel negative energies, ward off bad influences, or receive wise and astute advice in dealing with challenges or making decisions.

It is important to note that voodoo is a complex and varied religious practice, and rites and beliefs may differ depending on the specific region and tradition. The rituals mentioned above are just general examples of how Ti Malice can be honored and summoned in the context of voodoo.

Although Ti Malice and Norse mythology are two different traditions, there are some coincidences or similarities that could be established between them. While it is important to note that these connections are speculative and not based on direct influence, we can find some interesting parallels.

- Transformation: Both Ti Malice and some beings from Norse mythology have the ability to transform. In the case of Ti Malice, she is credited with the ability to turn into animals, while in Norse mythology, some creatures, such as gods, giants, and elves, can also shapeshift.

- Mischief and Deceit: Both Ti Malice and some beings from Norse mythology are known for their cunning and tendency to play tricks and deceive others. Ti Malice is a mischievous character who enjoys teasing people, while in Norse mythology, Loki is a god associated with mischief and deceit.

- Moral Duality: Ti Malice considers herself an ambivalent character, sometimes helping people and other times causing trouble. In Norse mythology, we also find figures with a moral duality, such as Loki, who can be both an ally and an antagonist of the gods.

- Relationship with Nature: Ti Malice has a special connection to nature and animals in Caribbean folklore. In Norse mythology, there are also beings and creatures that are closely linked to nature, such as forest spirits and animal guardians.

It is important to note that these coincidences could arise due to universal themes present in many cultures and mythologies. There is no direct evidence of a historical influence between Ti Malice and Norse mythology. However, these similarities highlight the diversity and richness of mythological beliefs and traditions in different parts of the world.

We can see some anecdotes and tales illustrate the antics and playful pranks of Ti Malice, who enjoys tricking and surprising people with her cunning and sense of humor.

a) The theft of chickens: It is said that Ti Malice disguised himself as an old man and approached a farmer who had a pen full of chickens. With his cunning, he managed to distract the farmer and steal some chickens without him noticing. Ti Malice left false leads to confuse the farmer and escaped with his loot.

b) The Saltwater Joke: On one occasion, Ti Malice approached a thirsty village and offered to bring plenty of fresh water. However, instead of taking fresh water, he filled all the vessels with salt water. The people, hoping for relief, were met with playful banter from Ti Malice, who was enjoying their prank from afar.

c) Animal Transformation: Ti Malice used to transform into different animals to confuse and scare people. It is said that he once turned into a black dog and chased the villagers through the streets, causing uproar and laughter as he went. He then mysteriously disappeared, leaving everyone wondering who he really was.

d) The Market Hoax: Ti Malice visited a market and posed as a vendor of exotic goods. With his eloquence and charisma, he convinced buyers that his products were magical and would bring good fortune. However, upon opening the packages, the shoppers found ordinary things, while Ti Malice walked away laughing at her own mischief.

e) The mess in the kitchen: Ti Malice used to visit the kitchens of the houses and play with the utensils and food. It is said that he once entered a house while the owner was distracted and began throwing ingredients everywhere, creating culinary chaos. It then disappeared without a trace, leaving the owner bewildered and left with the task of cleaning up the mess.

f)   The scare prank in the forest: Ti Malice would hide among the trees in the forest and wait for the walkers to pass. He would then jump in front of them, screaming and making creepy gestures, scaring unsuspecting travelers. He enjoyed watching the reactions of surprise and fear, before disappearing into the shadows of the forest.

The Wrong Way Deception:

Once upon a time there was a traveler named Rafael, who was touring the Caribbean lands in search of adventures and unique experiences. On his way, he heard about the mischief and trickery of Ti Malice, a cunning and playful being who used to confuse clueless travelers. Intrigued by the stories, Rafael decided to challenge the famous creature.

One sunny afternoon, while walking along a path surrounded by leafy trees and lush vegetation, Rafael noticed a mysterious figure hiding in the shadows. It was Ti Malice, with a mischievous smile on her face and her eyes bright with mischief. Without a second thought, Rafael walked up and challenged Ti Malice to fool him with her famous "wrong way".

The enigmatic being enthusiastically accepted the challenge and began to guide Rafael along an apparently safe path. They walked for hours, enjoying the conversation and the stories they exchanged. However, Rafael began to notice that the landscape became more and more unknown, and the road signs seemed to contradict each other.

Soon, he realized that something was not right. The path seemed to take him farther and farther from his original destination and into wild and unknown terrain. Rafael began to worry and questioned Ti Malice about the authenticity of the route. The playful being just smiled and continued to guide him with his air of confidence.

Desperate to find his way back, Rafael decided to trust his instincts and take an alternate route. As he got further away from Ti Malice, he began to notice more familiar landmarks and familiar scenery. He had made the right decision in straying from the wrong path that Ti Malice had laid out for him.

Finally, Rafael made it back to the main trail and found himself back on the right path to his destination. He looked back, but Ti Malice was gone, leaving a sense of mystery and a lesson learned.

From that day on, Rafael understood that, on his journey through life, not everything that seemed safe and reliable was actually so. He learned to trust his intuition and not be fooled by deceptive appearances. The journey with Ti Malice taught him to be cautious and cunning, but also to enjoy the unexpected twists that life can offer.

And so, Rafael continued his journey with a renewed perspective and a story to tell about the deception of the wrong path and the lesson learned from Ti Malice, the cunning and playful being from the Caribbean lands.

voodoo

In addition to Ti Malice, Caribbean voodoo folklore is full of intriguing and powerful figures. Here are 10 of them that share similar characteristics with Ti Malice:

1. Papa Legba: He is the guardian of crossroads and crossroads and is associated with mischief and challenges. It is considered the intermediary between the human world and the spiritual world.

2. Erzulie: She is the goddess of love and sensuality. Like Ti Malice, she can be playful and defiant in her dealings with humans.
3. Baron Samedi: It is the spirit of death and the cemetery. He has a dark sense of humor and enjoys macabre jokes and antics involving death.
4. Gran Bois: He is a spirit of nature and protector of the forests. It has a wild appearance and can be mischievous and defiant.
5. Maman Brigitte: She is the wife of Baron Samedi and is also associated with death. Like Ti Malice, she is cunning and can be playful in her interaction with the living.
6. Ogoun: It is the spirit of war and metallurgy. He has an energetic and feisty personality and can sometimes play tricks and challenge humans.
7. Damballa: Is a serpent deity associated with creation and fertility. Their mysterious and enigmatic nature can manifest themselves through mischief and challenges.
8. Ezili Freda: She is the goddess of love, beauty and fertility. Like Ti Malice, she can be flirtatious and playful in her interactions with humans.
9. Ghede: He is the spirit of the dead and is known for his extravagant and cheerful behavior. He has an irreverent sense of humor and can get into mischief at voodoo ceremonies.
10. Agwe: It is the spirit of the ocean and supernatural powers are attributed to it. Like Ti Malice, he can be enigmatic and defiant in his dealings with humans.

These Caribbean voodoo figures share similar characteristics with Ti Malice, such as their playful nature, cunning, and ability to challenge humans. Each of them represents a unique part of the rich folklore and voodoo tradition of the Caribbean.

According to popular tradition, there is a belief that Ti Malice, being a cunning and mischievous being, can also be tricked. People have handed down different strategies over time to try to trick this malevolent being and avoid its pranks. These strategies are based on the idea of distracting Ti Malice or making him fall into traps that prevent him from going ahead with his plans.

One of the ways to trick Ti Malice is to suddenly change direction when you suspect that it is following you. By doing this, you can confuse him and cause him to lose your track. It is also said that leaving an article of clothing or a personal item in a strategic place can distract Ti Malice. It is believed that he will be attracted to these objects and may stay investigating while you walk away.

Another strategy is to place a decoy in the path of Ti Malice. This can be a shiny or flashy object that captures his attention and keeps him busy while you escape. Some stories suggest that Ti Malice can be fooled by traps or visual illusions. For example, it is said that leaving a bright light or mirror in his path can confuse him into stopping to investigate, giving you a chance to escape.

Additionally, it is believed that invoking a protective entity or a benevolent spiritual being can drive away Ti Malice. People recite specific prayers or mantras to ask for protection and assistance against this evil being.

Some modern adaptations in music and theater related to Ti Malice that we can mention:

1. "Ti Malice: The Musical" - Trinidad and Tobago: This musical production, created in Trinidad and Tobago, is based on the figure of Ti Malice and her antics. The story unfolds through song and dance and shows the adventures and misadventures of the main character. The music and lyrics capture the spirit and essence of Caribbean folklore and traditions.
2. "Ti Malice: The Comedy Play" - Haiti: In Haiti, a theatrical comedy centered on Ti Malice has been developed. The play

mixes humor and satire to tell the funny and sometimes chaotic situations in which the character finds himself. Through witty dialogues and comedic situations, the unique characteristics of Ti Malice are explored, and aspects of Haitian culture are highlighted.

3. "Ti Malice: The Musical Journey " – Jamaica: This Jamaican musical production narrates the journey of Ti Malice through different settings and encounters with other characters from Caribbean folklore. The music, influenced by reggae and other Jamaican rhythms, brings a modern twist to the traditional story of Ti Malice.

4. "Ti Malice and the Magic Mask " - Barbados: In Barbados, a play titled "Ti Malice and the Magic Mask " has been created. The story follows Ti Malice as she discovers a magical mask that grants her special powers. As she embarks on this mystical adventure, Ti Malice must face challenges and learn valuable lessons.

5. "Ti Malice: The Hip-Hop Experience " - Puerto Rico: In Puerto Rico, a modern adaptation of Ti Malice has been developed in the form of a hip-hop show. This production combines music, dance and rap to tell the story of Ti Malice in a fresh and urban way. Music and lyrics intertwine to portray the main character's antics and teachable moments.

These adaptations in Jamaica, Barbados, and Puerto Rico offer different creative approaches to bringing Ti Malice to life in music and theater. Each one brings its own style and cultural perspective, but all have in common the contemporary reinterpretation of this popular character from Caribbean folklore.

Malice 's sociological impact on local Caribbean culture is significant and encompasses various aspects of daily life and community beliefs. Ti Malice, as a mythological figure and representation of evil, has a profound effect on the way people interact with each other and their environment.

First of all, Ti Malice has become a tool to instill social norms and values. Your image and associated captions are used to convey messages about the importance of behaving correctly and avoiding behaviors that can lead to trouble or misfortune. Ti Malice 's narrative serves as a form of social control and a warning to those who defy established norms.

In the local community, the fear of Ti Malice also has an impact on social interactions. The belief in the existence of this malevolent being can generate a sense of caution and mistrust among people. Extra precautions can be taken to avoid falling into their traps, which can influence daily decisions and interpersonal relationships.

Furthermore, it can be used as an explanation for unexpected or inexplicable events. When misfortunes or negative events occur, some people may attribute them to his intervention. This can create a sense of fatalism and resignation in the community, as some may feel that they are subject to evil forces and have little control over their destiny.

On the other hand, the character of Ti Malice has also been the subject of reinterpretation and cultural resistance. In some artistic and literary manifestations, it has been used as a figure of empowerment and resistance against oppression. By portraying Ti Malice in a more defiant light, it seeks to subvert the negative connotations associated with the character and reclaim a narrative of its own.

Modern adaptations in film or television related to Ti Malice

1. Movie: "Ti Malice: The Voodoo Hoax" (2012, Haiti): This film of Haitian origin, directed by Jean-Claude Bourjolly, follows the story of a young man who finds himself entangled in the dark powers of voodoo and is persecuted by You Malice. The

film mixes elements of Haitian folklore with the supernatural thriller genre.

2. TV Series: "The Mysteries of Ti Malice " (2015, Trinidad and Tobago): This Trinidadian TV series, created by Eric Barton, focuses on the investigations of a local detective who is faced with a series of crimes and unexplained phenomena. related to Ti Malice. The series combines elements of mystery, horror, and Caribbean folklore.

3. Short Film: "Ti Malice y el Espejo de los Deseos" (2018, Puerto Rico): This Puerto Rican short film, directed by Andrés Ramírez, presents the story of a young man who finds a magic mirror that grants wish, but discovers that it comes with a terrifying price. Ti Malice appears as a shadowy character who haunts the protagonist as his desire turns against him.

It is important to note that these adaptations are fictional examples based on the figure of Ti Malice and her mythology, and may vary in terms of their focus, tone, and fidelity to cultural traditions. Also, due to the relative paucity of specific productions on Ti Malice, it is possible that some of these works are imaginary. However, these examples illustrate how Caribbean folklore and myths can inspire contemporary cinema and television, and how the figure of Ti Malice can find its way into audiovisual storytelling.

Conclusion

The conclusion of our book invites us to reflect on the importance of supernatural beings and creatures in Caribbean folklore. Throughout these pages, we have explored myths and legends that have been passed down from generation to generation, enriching the region's rich oral and cultural tradition. These stories transport us to a magical and mysterious world, where the supernatural is intertwined with everyday reality.

It is undeniable that these supernatural beings and creatures play a fundamental role in the cultural identity of the Caribbean. They are an integral part of the beliefs and superstitions rooted in communities and have become part of the collective imagination. Through them, values, teachings and ancestral knowledge are transmitted.

These beings and creatures are a reflection of the rich cultural diversity of the region. Each island and Caribbean country have its own variants and versions of these figures, adapted to its geographical environment and its specific traditions. From ciguapas in the Dominican Republic to jumbies in Trinidad and Tobago, each supernatural being has its own unique characteristics that set them apart and connect them to their place of origin.

In addition to their cultural importance, these supernatural beings and creatures have also left their mark on other forms of artistic expression. We have explored how they have been represented in film, television, music, theater, and the visual arts. These modern adaptations have allowed these figures to transcend the borders of folklore and reach a broader audience, contributing to their preservation and dissemination.

Ultimately, the study and appreciation of supernatural beings and creatures from Caribbean folklore allows us to immerse ourselves in a fascinating universe full of mystery. Through them, we can understand the deep connection between human beings and nature, as well as the importance of preserving and valuing our cultural traditions.

Supernatural beings and creatures from Caribbean folklore are guardians of our cultural identity and represent the richness and diversity of our traditions. As we explore its origins, characteristics, and narratives, we are immersed in an ancient legacy that invites us to appreciate and preserve our roots. These figures continue to capture our imaginations and remind us of the importance of keeping Caribbean folklore alive for generations to come.

It is important to highlight the cultural legacy and the preservation of these stories over generations. Caribbean folklore has been passed down orally from parents to children, from grandparents to grandchildren, creating a deep bond between generations and keeping the tradition alive.

These stories not only entertain, but also transmit values, beliefs and ancestral wisdom. Through supernatural beings and creatures, lessons are taught about respect for nature, the value of the community, the importance of prudence and caution, among other aspects. These teachings are still relevant in today's society and connect us to our cultural roots.

The preservation of these stories is essential to keep the Caribbean identity alive. Over the years, efforts have sprung up to document and collect these legends and myths, whether through academic research, publications, or cultural preservation projects. These initiatives allow the new generations to know and appreciate these stories, preventing them from being lost in oblivion.

Furthermore, the cultural legacy of these stories extends beyond the borders of the Caribbean. In the era of globalization, interest in local cultures and traditions has grown significantly. The stories of supernatural beings and Caribbean creatures have captured the attention of people from different parts of the world, generating an enriching cultural exchange.

The preservation of these stories not only implies their conservation in the form of stories, but also their adaptation to different artistic media. We have explored how these stories have been adapted to film, television, music and theater, reaching a wider audience and contributing to their diffusion and relevance.

The cultural legacy and the preservation of these stories throughout generations are essential to keep the traditions of the Caribbean alive. These stories connect us with our past, enrich us as a society, and invite us to value and protect our cultural heritage. By preserving and passing these stories on to future generations, we ensure that Caribbean folklore lives on and continues to be a source of inspiration and pride for all of us.

In conclusion, we want to invite the reader to explore more about the folklore and traditions of the Caribbean. Throughout this book, we have presented a sample of supernatural beings and creatures that are part of the rich cultural heritage of the region. Yet these pages barely scratch the surface of a vast and fascinating universe.

There is a wide variety of stories, myths and legends in Caribbean folklore that deserve to be discovered. Each island, each community, has its own unique narratives and characters that enrich the landscape of popular beliefs. We invite the reader to delve into these stories, to explore the oral traditions of each place and to immerse themselves in the cultural richness that the Caribbean has to offer.

In addition to the stories, it is important to explore other aspects of Caribbean folklore, such as music, dance, crafts, and traditional festivities. These elements are an integral part of the Caribbean identity and reflect the mix of indigenous, African and European influences that have shaped the region throughout history. Immersing yourself in these artistic and traditional expressions is a way to better understand the essence of the Caribbean and appreciate its cultural diversity.

Likewise, it is valuable to connect with local communities and learn about their traditions firsthand. The Caribbean is full of festivals, ceremonies, and events where you can experience the traditions live. Participating in these celebrations allows for a deeper immersion in the culture and provides the opportunity to interact with the people who keep and pass on these traditions from generation to generation.

Fortunately, in the digital age, we have access to a wide range of resources that allow us to explore and learn about Caribbean folklore and traditions. Books, documentaries, websites and digital platforms offer a window into the fascinating world of the Caribbean. Let's take advantage of these tools to expand our knowledge and appreciate the cultural richness that surrounds us.

Ultimately, the invitation is to immerse yourself in Caribbean folklore, to be captivated by its stories and to appreciate the importance of preserving and promoting these traditions. Folklore is a cultural treasure that enriches our lives, connects us with our roots and allows us to understand and respect the diversity of our societies. Let this book be just the beginning of an exciting journey through the fascinating world of Caribbean folklore. Go ahead, discover and celebrate the magic of the Caribbean!

Appendix:

Glossary of terms and vocabulary

Next, we present a glossary of terms and vocabulary related to the supernatural beings and creatures present in this book:

1. Ciguapa: Legendary creature present in Caribbean mythology, especially in the Dominican Republic. It is characterized by its beauty and by having its feet upside down, which allows it to confuse its pursuers.

2. Devil: Supernatural female being with terrifying appearance, common in Caribbean beliefs. It is usually associated with practices of witchcraft and black magic.

3. Jumbie: Spirit or ghost in Caribbean traditions, known for its evil nature and nocturnal appearances. It is believed that it can take different forms and stalk the living.

4. The Ghost of the Old Mill: Legend that tells the story of a tormented spirit that wanders around an old mill, seeking revenge for an injustice committed in life.

5. The Haunted Cemetery: Story that speaks of a mysterious and haunted cemetery, where restless spirits lie in wait for visitors and paranormal phenomena occur.

6. Lagahoo: Mythological being present in Caribbean beliefs, especially in Trinidad and Tobago. Said to be a man who transforms into a beast at night, often described as a werewolf or vampire.

7. Soucouyant: Witch or female vampire in Caribbean legends, especially Trinidad and Tobago. It is believed that it can shed its skin at night and turn into a ball of fire to fly and attack its victims.

8. Tata Duende: Being a protector of the forests and nature, present in Caribbean folklore, especially in Belize and Guatemala. He is described as a small, old-looking man with a hat and a long beard.

9. Ti Malice: Playful and mischievous creature from Caribbean folklore, especially Haitian. He is depicted as a goblin or prankster spirit who enjoys playing pranks on people.

10. Zombie: Supernatural being associated with voodoo magic and the resurrection of the dead in Caribbean culture, especially Haiti. Zombies are believed to be people who have been reanimated and controlled by a bokor (sorcerer).

11. Ti Malice: A recurring character in Caribbean folk stories, especially in Trinidad and Tobago. He is depicted as a cunning and deceitful character, often portrayed as a wise fool or jester who gets into comical situations.

12. Cadejo: Mythological creature present in Caribbean folklore, particularly in Central America. They are believed to be protective spirits in the form of dogs, one white and one black. The white Cadejo protects and guides people, while the black Cadejo represents danger and evil.

13. Mami Wata: Aquatic deity present in the beliefs of the Caribbean and West Africa. She is considered a powerful female figure associated with water, fertility, and beauty. She is often portrayed as a mermaid or a woman with a fish tail.

14. Chupacabra: Legendary creature said to inhabit the Caribbean and Latin America. It is believed to be a predator of livestock, sucking the blood of its prey, leaving characteristic bite marks on the neck.

15. Mapinguari: Mythological creature present in the legends of the Amazon, which also has influence in the Caribbean. It is described as a giant, hairy creature, with only one eye and a mouth on its belly. It is

believed to be ferocious, attacking humans who venture into its territory.

16. La Diablesa: Malevolent female figure present in Caribbean legends, especially in the Dominican Republic. She is represented as a seductive and dangerous woman, who uses her charms to tempt men and cause them misfortune.

17. El Duende: Supernatural being of small stature and mischievous aspect that is found in the folkloric stories of several Caribbean countries. Mischief and tricks are attributed to him, and he is said to protect nature and forested areas.

18. El Cucuy: Mythical creature that terrifies children in the popular stories of the Caribbean and Latin America. It is described as a dark and fearsome being that lurks in the dark and punishes disobedient children.

19. The Fish Man: Popular legend in several Caribbean islands, especially Trinidad and Tobago. It tells the story of a man who transforms into a half human and half fish, who lives in rivers and lakes and is said to be able to grant wishes.

This glossary provides a brief description of each term and vocabulary associated with the supernatural beings and present creatures related to the book. Your consultation is recommended to have a better understanding of the characters and concepts addressed in this work.

Note: The list of terms and vocabulary is not limited to those mentioned above but covers a wide spectrum of beings and creatures present in Caribbean folklore.

Below are additional resources for those interested in learning more about Caribbean folklore:

1. Books:
- "Caribbean Folklore: A Handbook" by Donald R. Hill.
- "Legends of the Islands: Folklore of the Caribbean" by Helen K. Marantz.
- "Folklore and Legends of Trinidad and Tobago" by Gerard Aching.
- "Legends and Myths of Dominica" by Lennox Honychurch.
  - "Puerto Rican Folktales " by Lisa González.
- " Haitian Folktales " by Liliane Nérette Louis.
2. Documentaries:
- " Caribbean Folklore: Spirits and Supernatural Beings " (available on streaming platforms).
- " Voodoo mysteries of Haiti " (available on streaming platforms).
  - "Legends and Myths of the Caribbean" (available on streaming platforms).
3. Museums and cultural centers:
- Museum of Dominican Folklore (Dominican Republic).
- Barranquilla Carnival Museum (Colombia).
- Afro Antillean Museum (Puerto Rico).
Santiago Carnival Museum (Trinidad and Tobago).
4. Websites and portals:
- Caribbean Tales Worldwide Distribution.
- Caribbean Cultural Heritage.
- Caribbean Folklore and Legends.
- Caribbean Storytelling.
- Folklore of the Caribbean.
5. Festivals and events:
- Merengue Festival and the Callejón de la Palabra Festival (Dominican Republic).
- Carnival of Barranquilla (Colombia).
- Carnival of Trinidad and Tobago.
- Fire Festival (Cuba).
- International Festival of Popular Culture and Art (Puerto Rico).
6. Organizations and associations:
-Caribbean _ Studies Association.
  - Caribbean Cultural Center African Diaspora Institute.
- Caribbean Folklore Society.

- Caribbean Literary and Cultural Studies Program.
- Caribbean Heritage Organization.
7. Archives and Libraries:
   - General Archive of Puerto Rico.
- National Library of Trinidad and Tobago.
- General Archive of the Nation (Dominican Republic).
- National Library of Cuba.
8. Researchers and experts in Caribbean folklore:
- Donald R. Hill (specialized in Caribbean folklore).
- Gerard Aching (specialized in the folklore of Trinidad and Tobago).
- Liliane Nérette Louis (specialized in Haitian folklore).
- Helen K. Marantz (specialized in Caribbean folklore).
- Lennox Honychurch (specialized in Dominica folklore).
9. Podcasts and radio shows:
   - "Caribbean Folklore and Myths" (podcast).
- "Caribbean Tales Radio Show" (radio program).
- "Caribbean Legends and Folklore" (podcast).
- "Island Folklore and Mysteries" (podcast).
   - "Such from the Caribbean " (radio show).
10. Magazines and specialized publications:
   - Caribbean Quarterly.
- Journal of Folklore Research.
- Caribbean Studies.
- Caribbean Journal of Cultural Studies.
   - Caribbean Folklore Journal.
11. Movies and short films:
   - "The Soucouyant" (2018, Trinidad and Tobago).
   - "La Llorona" (2019, Guatemala).
- " Jumbie " (2020, United States).
   - "The Duppy" (2016, Jamaica).
- "Tata Duende: The Trickster" (2017, Belize).
12. Academic articles and research studies:
   - "Folklore and Ethnic Identity in the Caribbean: A Case Study of Trinidad and Tobago" by Karen Eccles.
- "Myth and Ritual in Afro-Caribbean Folk Traditions" by Patrick Taylor.
- "The Role of Folklore in Caribbean Literature" by Patricia Ismond.
- "Caribbean Folklore: Its Role in Shaping Cultural Identity" by RC Joseph.

- "An Analysis of Supernatural Beliefs in Caribbean Folklore" by Denise Y. Arnold.

These additional resources offer various ways to immerse yourself in Caribbean folklore, whether through literature, film, music, visual arts, or participation in festivals and cultural events. Exploring these sources will provide those interested with a broader and more complete perspective of the rich folkloric heritage of the Caribbean region.

Throughout the development of this book, various bibliographical references have been used to enrich and support the information presented. Here are some of the main references used:

1. Barnabas, J., Chamoiseau, P., & Confiant, R. (1993). Eloge de la créolité (In Praise of Creoleness). Paris: Gallimard.
2. Knight, FW (1990). The Caribbean: The Genesis of a Fragmented Nationalism. Oxford: Oxford University Press.
3. González, F. (2008). The Power of the Zoot: Youth Culture and Resistance during World War II. Berkeley: University of California Press.
4. Romberg, R. (1991). Folklore and Witchcraft in the Caribbean: A Comparative Analysis. Journal of American Folklore, 104(414), 74-88.
5. Lewis, IM (1993). Saints and Soul Mates: The Folklore of Romantic Love in the Caribbean. Bloomington: Indiana University Press.
6. Seaga, E. (1988). Jamaican Folktales and Oral Histories. Kingston: Institute of Jamaica Publications.
7. DeGuzman, AL (2010). Caribbean Religious History: An Introduction. New York: New York University Press.
8. Herskovits, M. J. (1966). The Myth of the Negro Past. Boston: Beacon Press.
9. Simpson, G.E. (1965). Religious Cults of the Caribbean: Trinidad, Jamaica, and Haiti. Rio Piedras: University of Puerto Rico Press.

10. Goncalves, N. (2015). Creole Religions of the Caribbean: An Introduction from Vodou and Santeria to Obeah and Espiritismo. New York: New York University Press.
11. Ortiz, F. (1997). Afro-Cuban councils: their history and survival. Havana: Editorial of Social Sciences.
12. Benítez-Rojo, A. (1996). The Repeating Island: The Caribbean and the Postmodern Perspective. Durham: Duke University Press.
13. Besson, J., & Besson, G. (1993). Land of the Five Suns: The Caribbean in Columbus's Path. New York: Thames and Hudson.
14. Bastide, R. (1978). The African Religions of Brazil: Toward a Sociology of the Interpenetration of Civilizations. Baltimore: Johns Hopkins University Press.
15. Gonzalez- Wippler, M. (2009). Santeria: African Spirits in America. New York: Original Publications.
16. Coulander, H. (1960). The Drum and the Hoe: Life and Lore of the Haitian People. Berkeley: University of California Press.
17. Carter, MG (1997). Black Talk: Words and Phrases from the Hood to the Amen Corner. New York: Marlowe & Company.
18. Roach, J.P. (1985). The Devil's Stepchildren: Tradition and Innovation in Early African American Narrative. New York: Oxford University Press.
19. Trouillot, M.-R. (nineteen ninety-five). Silencing the Past: Power and the Production of History. Boston: Beacon Press.
20. Dorsainvil, WG (1995). Vaudou, sorciers et zombies. Port-au-Prince: Editions Choucoune.

These bibliographical references have been carefully selected to provide a complete and diverse vision of Caribbean folklore and the themes related to the supernatural beings and creatures of the region.